MY FA...
FRIEND

A Comedy

by

CHARLES LAURENCE

LONDON

NEW YORK   TORONTO   SYDNEY   HOLLYWOOD

MY FAT FRIEND

First presented by Michael Codron Ltd at the Globe
Theatre, London, in December 1972, with the following
cast of characters:

Henry	Kenneth Williams
Vicky	Jennie Linden
James	John Harding
Tom	Bernard Holly

The play directed by Eric Thompson
Setting by Alan Pickford

The action takes place in Vicky's house and bookshop
in Hampstead

ACT I
    Scene 1   An August morning
    Scene 2   That evening
    Scene 3   The next day

ACT II
    Scene 1   Sunday, four months later
    Scene 2   Christmas Eve
    Scene 3   Later the same evening

Time – the present

ACT I

SCENE 1

The ground floor of a small terraced Victorian house on a hill. An August morning

The setting shows the kitchen, living area, a small landing with a door to the bathroom, and the stairs to the bedrooms. Opening on to the living area is a door to the bookshop and a window which also opens on to the shop. This is partly covered by a curtain on a pole. The living area has a small sofa, an armchair and a coffee-table. There are lots of bookcases, a transistor radio, and a telephone: stripped floorboards with a centre carpet. The furniture is mostly second-hand bargains of many periods chosen with individual taste and affection. The effect is bright and warm. The kitchen has a glass conservatory at the back, with a door leading to a garden/yard; down stage from the cooking area are three chairs set round a pine table, and a "Mucha" poster

When the CURTAIN *rises the table in the dining area is set for breakfast. The shop and bathroom doors are closed. James, a tall Scots, quiet, passive youth of eighteen is reading a book and drinking coffee. Henry clatters down the stairs. He is in his early forties, an experienced face giving the lie to a slim, lithe body. His tie is hanging loose around his neck, and he carries his jacket and briefcase*

James 'Morning.
Henry 'Morning, James. (*He puts his coat on the sofa. He comes into the room, stops, mutters, "I'm going mad", turns and goes up to the landing and tries the bathroom door which is locked. He sighs, rattles the door and waits for a second*)
Henry For God's sake, Vicky, if you're dead give us some sign.
Vicky (*off*) What do you want?
Henry What do you think I want? I want to pee, you idiot.
Vicky (*off*) I'm doing my face.
Henry Not in the loo, surely? Come on. I've reached the cross-legged stage.
Vicky Hold it.
Henry Hold it. I'm a queen, dear, not a camel. Open up. (*He rattles the door vigorously and bangs on the glass panes*)
Vicky (*off*) Stop it.
Henry I can't, I shall have to do it through the keyhole.
Vicky (*off*) Go away.

Henry Come on, Vicky, be a sport, unlock the door. I give you full permission to modestly avert your eyes.

Vicky (*off*) It would put me off my breakfast.

Henry King Kong wouldn't put you off your breakfast. Look, stop playing about, I'm desperate.

Vicky (*off*) Then use your imagination

Henry gives the door a final little kick

Henry And don't think I won't.

Henry goes out of the kitchen door to have a "pee", peers through the kitchen window, returns, washes his hands at the sink, and goes to the mirror on the dresser to do up his tie

Henry We need a bigger bird bath.

James is still seated at the table, eating and reading

James Do we?

Henry And how are you this bright morning, James Anderson? Any erotic dreams to report?

James No, I'm sorry. None.

Henry You really ought to see a doctor, it's not natural for a boy of your age. Must be just the generation gap, I suppose, but when I was eighteen my nights were full—Tyrone Power, Robert Taylor and the young Cooper—Gladys, of course! Ah, happy days.

James The tea's made.

Henry sits at the table. He picks up the toast-rack

Henry What's this?

James A toast-rack—I got it from War on Want.

Henry Mmm, very worthy but toast should really be served from a crisp linen napkin, and it should be hot, piping hot—this little lot's barely tepid.

Henry starts buttering his toast, then helps himself to marmalade

James It was good when I made it. You shouldn't spend so much time in the bathroom.

Henry Chance would be a fine thing. Vicky's been stuck in there for the last half-hour slashing her wrists with a rubber razor.

James Are you in for lunch?

Henry Why? Oh, of course, it's Saturday. Let me think—er—no, I've got a driving lesson this afternoon, I'll go on from work.

James How is the driving?

Henry Mr Wilson's quite pleased with me, I think. Says I'm erratic.

James Oh. Is that good?

Henry It means that I'm an excellent driver from time to time.

James They do *say* you need a lesson for every year of your life.

Henry Thank you. That's about the bitchiest thing that anybody's ever said to me.

James Will you pass your test, do you think?

Henry I've got that all worked out. I'm going to write ETTA after Henry in my driving licence and take it as a nun.

James What good will that do?

Henry I shall have a completely clear road. Have you ever seen anyone flash or honk at a nun? Or cut in on them? No. It'll be a piece of cake. Sister Henrietta will sit there smiling benignly, very closely shaven, nodding her wimple every now and then—the rest of the traffic will vanish. My only trouble will be to stop the beads getting tangled around the gear lever.

James You might get arrested.

Henry I would plead religious mania.

James goes back to his book

Vicky comes out of the bathroom and into the living-room. She is small, pretty, twenty-nine, and about three stone overweight. She wears a blue dress and stops for a second to pull at it

James sees her and rises to put milk on the stove

James 'Morning.

Henry You've said that.

James I'm talking to Vicky.

Henry Oh, she's out, is she? Well, watch yourself she's extremely tetchy.

Vicky Who's bloody tetchy?

Vicky picks up the cigarettes and matches from the coffee-table, and sits at the dining-table

Henry You, my little pixie. What happened, crash out of bed the wrong side this morning, did we?

James Did you sleep well, Vicky?

Vicky Not very. Well, Henry, why aren't you rushing?

Vicky starts to pour out tea

Henry Because it's not ladylike—what are you talking about?

Vicky I thought you were dying to go?

Henry Oh, that. Darling, I took your advice. I've been.

Vicky You've what!

Henry points at the sink

Henry In that receptacle you laughingly call a bird bath. I mean if an eagle escaped from the zoo . . .

Vicky Oh, you filthy pig.

Henry Don't fuss. We may get a sparrow flitting about with chic bleached feathers.

Vicky How could you, oh, how could you?

Henry I stood on tiptoe, went up on my points.

Vicky And how could you, James Anderson, let him do it?

James I'm sorry, I had no idea . . .

Henry What could he have done, anyway, the little Dutch boy routine?

Vicky That was a dyke not a raving, screaming, insane elderly poof.

Henry Vicky, do sit down, have your breakfast and stop carrying on, Jesus loves you! All of you.

Vicky pours cornflakes. James gets warm milk and pours it over them

Vicky It's pitiful, an infantile desire to shock, pitiful.

James Can I do anything to help?

Henry No, carry on with your well-known impersonation of a Scottish *au pair*. Vicky is merely indulging in typical female envy.

Vicky Huh! What could I, or anybody else for that matter, possibly envy you?

Henry Well, for a start, I doubt if you could have managed to pee in a bird bath without the aid of some helpful, passing crane driver.

Pause

James I'll make some fresh toast.

James takes the toast-rack into the kitchen and makes toast

Vicky You're going to be a really foul old man, Henry.

Henry I hope so, I do hope so. It's the only kind to be. (*He holds out a sugar basin*) Sugar? Or are we indulging ourselves in yet another futile diet this week?

Vicky grabs angrily at the sugar basin that Henry is holding out and spills half of it

Vicky (*near to tears*) Oh, you sod!

Henry Sorry, love.

James No harm done. I'll clear up. Have your flakes, Vicky, or they'll get soggy.

James begins to sweep the sugar off the cloth. Vicky eats in silence, eyes down. Henry looks at James and pulls a "what's up with her" face. James gives a little nod towards Vicky and goes to the sink with the cloth, sugar and paper

Henry It's a lovely sunny day. Blue sky.

Pause

You're looking very nice, Victoria—very nice.

Vicky And what does that mean?

Henry What can it mean apart from what I said?

Vicky Lots of things.

Henry Such as?

Vicky Let me see. It could mean that—er—you wanted to borrow some more money . . .

Henry smiles and leans back

Or that you wanted to sleep with me . . .

Henry mockingly covers his mouth with his hand

Or even more unlikely . . .

Henry Never, what could be more unlikely than that?

Vicky You could in your clumsy, constipated way, be apologizing.

Henry laughs

Henry Fantasy. Madame Bovary meets Walter Mitty. All I meant was that your dress is an attractive shade of blue and that it suits you.

Vicky My God! You don't give up, do you? Prod and poke and pick at the same scab with your grimy little fingers until it turns into a running sore.

Henry Urgh! Please, I'm eating.

Vicky Try choking.

James brings fresh toast to the table, and the paper

James Here you are, Vicky. Marmalade?

Vicky Thank you, James.

James clears the bowl and hot milk jug to the kitchen

Henry What's got into you this morning, apart from a rather large bowl of cornflakes?

Vicky Henry, please, do me a favour, don't attempt to put that raddled old face into the shapes of innocence—the effect is positively macabre, like putting a chintz cover on an old boot.

Henry (*quietly*) Let's not get personal, Vicky. Remember, I'm much better at it than you.

Vicky Personal! And what have you been doing ever since I came down?

Henry Trying, in the face of great difficulty I might add, to make a little polite conversation to aid your gastric juices.

Vicky There you go again. You can't resist the snide remark.

Jame sits at the table

Henry I give up. James Anderson, have I given any more offence than usual?

James I haven't really been listening, but that is a very bonny dress you're wearing, Vicky.

Vicky Don't you start for Christ's sake.

Henry rises dramatically, arms outstretched

Henry Hold everything, hold everything. I've had a glimmer. (*He peers at Vicky*) It's all coming back, my God, yes, it is. Of course it is.

James What is it?

Henry That. That is the sweet little Alice blue gown, isn't it?

Vicky Do stop it, Henry.

She reaches for a piece of toast

Henry Quick, James Anderson, this is an emergency, red alert. Action stations, please, clear the table, lock the larder and slip the key down your virgin jeans—I'll recover it later. (*He throws the cornflake packet at James, picks up and hugs the marmalade and removes the toast from Vicky's hand*)

Vicky If you don't put all that back at once I shall scream.

Henry My God, withdrawal symptoms already—I wonder, would a rubber bone keep her happy?

James What's going on?

Henry Are you blind or just simple? Can't you see? She is wearing the fat dress!

Vicky puts a cigarette in her mouth. Henry puts out his hand

Wait a minute, are you going to smoke that or eat it?

Vicky strikes a match under his hand

(*Angrily*) Hey, you could have burnt me.

Vicky All right. You've made your point, had your fun, so why don't you ponce off to work?

Henry I can't leave you in the ample clutches of the fat dress.

James It's a bonny outfit, why do you call it fat?

Vicky That'll do.

Henry You really don't know?

Jame shakes his head

He doesn't know. That means it's at least eighteen months since you had to wear it. Vicky, James Anderson has been with us a year and a half.

Vicky You don't have to remind me. (*She lights her cigarette*)

Henry Good girl, have a fag, cut the appetite. Kill the pangs—here, have two.

Vicky slaps the packet out of his hand

Ow, that hurt.

Vicky At last, a ray of sunshine.

James (*rising*) Excuse me, I'd better go and open the shop.

Henry Stay where you are. She deserves public humiliation. It'll help her, I must be cruel . . .

Vicky Surprise, surprise.

Henry To be kind.

Vicky opens the newspaper and feigns indifference. Henry stalks round her

Victoria Hope, bookseller—rare bookseller and spinster of this parish, is wearing her last resort. This "bonny outfit" as you so elegantly described it, James Anderson, usually hangs ominously at the far end of her wardrobe, shrouded with horror, reeking of despair—avoided by moths and simple country folk after nightfall. It is a legend in its own time.

Vicky Oh. Really!

Henry Hush. For—for when the said Victoria Hope is forced to cover herself with this gross garment it means one thing and one thing only. It signifies to the world that everything else she possesses is too small for her to struggle into. In other words—she's been eating like a pig and made herself too bloody fat again.

Vicky Beautifully put.

Henry Thank you.

James But . . .

Henry Yes? Don't be shy.

James Vicky isn't fat.

Henry and Vicky turn and gaze at him with astonishment. Henry taps one of his ears

Henry I must get a new battery for this thing.

James She's not, not really.

Vicky What on earth am I then?

James You're—the butcher always says you're well-upholstered.

Henry goes into the living area

Vicky Oh, thank you, thank you very much. Made my day that has. How super, some cross-eyed git thinks I'm well-upholstered. What does he think I am, some kind of sofa for Christ's sake?

Henry Steady, old girl, you'll bust a spring.

Vicky rises

Vicky I've never heard of anything so foul and obscene.

James He means well, he smiles when he says it.

Vicky I bet he does, the bastard. Well-upholstered, bloody hell! (*She throws the newspaper in the air and goes to the living area*) Well-upholstered, Jesus!

Vicky exits upstairs

James picks up and folds the newspaper

Henry I don't think you should have said that.

James I only repeated what . . .

Henry I'm surprised at you, James Anderson. It was extremely cruel and thoughtless. I don't understand how you can behave like that, I was always taught to respect other people's feelings.

James But it was true.

Henry That makes it worse. You have got a lot to learn.

James What was so dreadful? I don't understand.

Henry Difficult to explain to a foreigner, tiny nuances of language. (*He sits on the sofa and puts files into his briefcase*) Vicky's an honest lass, why else would she keep a full-length mirror in her bedroom? God, if I was that size, I'd have a Tom Thumb looking-glass for plucking my eyebrows with and nothing else. Fat is a good honest Anglo-Saxon word, well-upholstered is an evasion, an absolutely evil phrase and you should go and wash your mouth out with porridge.

James But you say the most terrible things to her all the time.

Henry That's different, she's used to it. If I stopped she'd think she had cancer or acne. Besides, I'm fond of her.

James So am I.

Henry Yes, but you don't show it. You don't show anything, in fact, that's why I said you should see a doctor.

James I'd better go and apologize.

James moves to go upstairs

Henry Leave it, you'll only make it worse.

James goes to the table, puts everything on a tray and clears it to the kitchen

Basically, it's all your fault.

James In what sense?

Henry Your cooking, that's the coloured person in the woodpile.

James Vicky likes my cooking.

Henry Too bloody much. She never stops eating, you never stop cooking —it's a vicious circle. The only way to break it would be for me to take over the catering and that I won't do 'cause it would ruin my hands and turn my rings black.

James You don't wear any rings.

James does a final tidy and puts the chairs straight

Henry That is immaterial.

Henry picks his jacket off the sofa and gives it to James to hold out for him

Henry I must get off to work. Enjoy your day with madam.

James Henry, why don't you take the morning off?

Henry James Anderson, are you propositioning me at last?

James It's Saturday, you don't have to go in.

Henry Yes, I do, I need the overtime.

James I never know how to deal with Vicky when she's in a bad mood.

Henry It won't last, she's a sensible creature at heart. Look, you go and open the shop and don't worry your tartan head, I'll smooth her down.

James Thanks.

Vicky comes down the stairs, munching and with a huge box of chocolates in her hand

Vicky, I'm truly . . .

Vicky Isn't anybody going to work today? I'm not running a charity here, you know.

Vicky pushes Henry out of the way; he goes to the dining area and puts his briefcase on the table. Vicky goes to the sofa. Henry gives James a nod

James exits to the shop

Vicky mechanically eats another chocolate. Henry goes to the living area

Henry You've upset poor James Anderson dreadfully.
Vicky Do him good. Shake his liver up a bit.
Henry Is that remark scientifically sound?

Vicky does not answer

You might very well enjoy life as a sofa—depends who sat on you, of course.
Vicky (*coldly*) Would you knit me loose covers every spring?

Vicky resumes her pattern of eating, removing the top layer

Henry Eating chocolates can be habit forming.
Vicky Now he tells me.
Henry You'll get spots.
Vicky Hurrah!
Henry Big, fat, greasy spots.
Vicky Naturally, I'd look silly with thin spots.
Henry And nasty side effects, like getting even fatter.
Vicky Who cares?
Henry I don't, but you should.
Vicky Why?
Henry You run a bookshop not a circus.

Vicky slams down the box

Vicky I've had enough, I don't need to take this, it's my house. Get out. Get out and stay out. I'm giving you notice to quit.
Henry Oh no, not again—couldn't I be shot at dawn for a change?

Henry sits

A pale yellow sky and a firing squad of divine raw recruits who refuse to . . .
Vicky I'm serious, pack your poofy bags and go. Immediately.
Henry Do make up your mind.
Vicky Bugger off. (*She makes a "V" sign*)
Henry Do that again.
Vicky What? Why?
Henry It's the best imitation of Winston Churchill I've ever seen.
Vicky Go. Go. Go.
Henry I would, if I thought for one minute that you could manage without me.
Vicky Oh, that's rich. You're a retarded, emotional cripple, Henry, you couldn't support pussy.
Henry Very likely, dear, but I do have my uses.
Vicky So do maggots—and vultures, they pick bones clean.
Henry Sounds exactly what you need. Why not try Nature's way of slimming? Hire a friendly vulture and get rid of those unsightly bulges fast. "There's not much of me left now", says Victoria Hope, known as Old One Eye to her chums.

Vicky Urgh, you're disgusting.

Henry I know, but who else could stop you stuffing yourself with chocolates without using force or calling in the United Nations?

Vicky I probably wouldn't want to eat so much if—if I lived on my own.

Henry rises

Henry Come off it, girl. If you had to rely on your own tiny will-power, you wouldn't be able to get round the stairs in a couple of months. They'd have to hoist you up and down from the window like a grand piano. Actually, that's not a bad idea, we could sell tickets. (*He picks up the box of chocolates and offers it to her*) Go on, grow.

Vicky takes the box and tipping it up, bangs it down on Henry's head

Vicky Pig!

Pause, then Henry removes the box from his head

Henry I think I've got a marzipan crescent lodged in my ear. Would you care to check?

Vicky You idiot.

They fall giggling into each other's arms

Vicky (*breaking away*) Oh God, Henry, what am I going to do, it's all so depressing.

Henry Have an unhappy love affair and pine away the pounds.

Vicky I eat more when I'm sad. I don't even know I'm doing it till I catch sight of myself in a mirror, munching—at the end of the day my jaws ache.

Henry Then have a happy love affair.

Vicky Mmm, yes. I'll order one from Harrods.

Henry Why don't you bed James Anderson?

Vicky Don't be silly.

Henry He's handy, always on the premises and besides the exercise will do you good.

Vicky But would it be happy or unhappy?

Henry Fifty-fifty chance: he's a totally unknown quantity.

Vicky Is he? Totally?

Henry Yes.

Vicky I had wondered.

Henry How delicate of you not to ask.

Vicky I wasn't really all that interested.

Henry How rude.

Vicky Sorry. (*She laughs and leans against him*)

James Anderson opens the shop door

James Er—Vicky?

Vicky What do you want, you gorgeous highland hunk?

Henry Oooah, you're all right here, mate.

James Yes, I er—that is—we're a bit short on change, can I go round to George's?
Vicky Yes, of course. Go on, I'm just coming.
James I'll be as quick as I can.

James exits

Vicky No, I don't think it would work, he'd keep apologizing all the time.

The shop bell jangles. Henry goes for his briefcase

Henry I must go and brighten my office. I think I'll look in on that butcher on the way, he might be just what you're looking for.
Vicky Wait till you see him.
Henry You can't afford to be scornful. He obviously fancies you and he's accustomed to handling large chunks of meat. What could be better?

Vicky blows a raspberry at him

Vicky Get off, Henry.
Henry Fruit, that's the answer, eat fruit.
Vicky I hate fruit.
Henry All the better.

Henry blows a kiss and exits, leaving the door into the shop ajar

Vicky picks up the remains of the chocolate box, takes it to the kitchen and chucks it in the pedal bin. Passing the table she picks up an apple in the kitchen, takes a bite, chews and pulls a face. She feels her body despondently, draws a sudden deep breath and begins to do a few basic P.T. exercises with difficulty and determination

Vicky is attempting to touch her toes when Tom looks in from the shop door. Tom is in his early thirties, almost Mr Average, quietly good-looking, sun-tanned. He is carrying a book

Tom sees Vicky, who stretches up and goes down again in another vain attempt. Tom opens his mouth to speak, thinks better of it, begins to go

Vicky Come on, come on.

Tom stops and turns round

Bloody hell, my arms are too short.

She straightens up and feels her back. Tom knocks on the door. Vicky wheels round

What the—what do you want?

Tom holds out the book

Tom A book—from the tray outside the shop.
Vicky Oh, well, this part is private, very private.

Tom I'm sorry, but there was no-one in the shop. I do apologize for startling you.

Vicky That's all right, it's me. I'm a bit jumpy this morning. How much is it?

Tom I couldn't find the price.

Vicky Let me have a look.

Vicky reaches for the book. Between them they drop the book. Tom hurriedly bends and picks it up. The cover tears away from the book. Vicky takes the book. She looks through it

Gosh, it has been here a long time. Five shillings, reduced to two-and-six, reduced to ten p. What is it?

Tom *Life on the Persian Frontier.*

Vicky This must have been one of my father's books, he was mad about old travel books, filled the house with them.

Tom Really? Do you have any more?

Vicky I don't think so, I sent crateloads off to auction after he died. Though wait, there might be some on those lower shelves, if you'd care to look.

Tom Thank you very much, I will. Very kind of you. (*He goes to the bookshelves she points out, and squats to look at the books*)

Vicky goes to the table for cigarettes

Vicky If you find anything, bring it through to the shop.

Tom OK. Oh dear . . .

Vicky What's the matter?

Tom I've trodden on something—something soft. (*He stands balanced on one foot*)

Vicky goes over to him

Vicky Let me see. How extraordinary, a squashed lemon cream. I wonder how that got there?

Tom (*hopping*) Do you have a piece of paper? I don't want to mess your floor up.

Vicky Give me the shoe, I'll clean it off.

Tom No, really, I don't want to put you to . . .

Vicky It's all right, I'm insured, hand it over.

Tom slips off his shoe and gives it to her

Tom I'm being a nuisance.

Vicky All part of the service, you carry on.

Tom sits on the floor and begins to browse through the books. Vicky takes the shoe to the kitchen and wipes it with some damp kitchen paper

Persia is called something else now, isn't it?

Tom Yes, they changed the name, to Iran.

Vicky What a shame, Persia sounds so wildly mysterious and romantic.

Tom It's an interesting country. I've got to spend the next four months there.

Vicky Lucky you, four months, not a holiday, surely?

Tom No, my company's sending me out to look for oil around the Caspian.

Vicky goes into the living area

Vicky Ah, now tell me something. How do you go about looking for oil, I presume you don't wander about with a twig like a water diviner?

Tom (*laughing*) I wish I could, it would be a lot easier. No, I'm a geologist, I have to study a lot of boring things like strata and inclines and synclines.

Vicky That sounds very clever and completely baffling. Any luck? (*She crosses back to the kitchen*)

Tom Not yet, but it's a promising collection.

James Anderson enters with a loaded carrier bag and stops when he sees Tom

James Oh, sorry . . .

Tom Hello.

Vicky At last. What took you so long, James Anderson?

James gives a puzzled glance at Tom sitting on the floor and goes to the kitchen

James I thought I'd do a quick shop for supper. (*He leans close to her*) Who's that?

Vicky A customer.

James Have you noticed he's only wearing one shoe?

Vicky Maybe he's a Moslem, half a Moslem.

Vicky, with Tom's shoe, goes to the living area

Do we have any of my father's old travel books in the shop, James Anderson?

Tom Or old guide books?

James No, I don't think so.

Vicky Could you be an angel and check?

James Yes, of course. (*He moves towards the shop*)

Vicky hands Tom his shoe

Tom Thank you very much.

Vicky We pride ourselves on our service. Would you like my assistant to cut your toe-nails?

Tom smiles and shakes his head

James exits quickly into the shop

Tom You know, I still always expect booksellers to be crabby, Dickensian old gentlemen with half spectacles. (*He pulls a battered book from the shelves*)

Vicky You should have met my father, he even used to smell of books.

Tom This is fascinating, a Michelin guide to Istanbul published nineteen-thirty-one.

Vicky How's your French?

Tom Good enough for guide books and menus. Was your father a great traveller?

Vicky Only in his imagination. You know, journeys on the Orient Express with beautiful lady spies.

Tom That's something I've missed out on, so far.

Vicky Yes, well. You keep the books. (*She moves away*)

Tom How much do I owe you?

Vicky I don't know, they're both so battered, should have gone to a jumble sale ages ago. Tell you what, have them as a *bon voyage* present.

Tom No, I couldn't possibly . . .

Vicky Sorry, they're not for sale.

Tom But . . .

Vicky It's all a clever ploy really to make you feel guilty and buy more, that's how we get most of our trade.

Tom I should have thought you yourself were the main attraction.

Vicky goes quiet

Vicky Would you?

Tom Yes, indeed.

Vicky I said you could have the books.

Tom I meant what I said.

Vicky I don't have any illusions about myself. I know what I look like.

Tom You've been very helpful and pleasant to deal with and—and you are pretty.

Vicky I know, pretty fat.

Tom I wouldn't say that.

Vicky What would you say then?

Tom (*embarrassed*) Er—well—I . . .

Vicky I'm sorry, that was unfair of me. Look, just take the books.

Tom I still don't feel right about accepting them.

Vicky If it worries you, put some money in the Barnardo box—last time it was emptied they got eleven pence and two fag ends.

Tom I'll try and surprise them. Thank you again. Would you do me another favour?

Vicky If I can.

Tom Are you free for dinner tonight?

Vicky No, you don't have to . . .

Tom Please, I'm off into the wilds first thing in the morning, you can't refuse.

Vicky It's—it's terribly nice of you but, no, I can't.

Tom Very well then, blackmail—no dinner, no books.

Vicky That's silly.

Tom I agree, so I'll call for you at seven. Is there a door at the side?
Vicky No, we extended the shop, the bell's on the left by . . .
Tom I'll find it, do a bit of prospecting. Is it a deal?
Vicky If you like.

He holds out his hand. Vicky takes it

Tom Tom Reynolds.
Vicky Victoria Hope.
Tom 'Till this evening, I'll look forward to it. Good-bye, Miss Hope.
Vicky 'Bye.

Tom exits

Vicki stands thinking for a moment, then goes over to the coffee-table where she left her apple. She picks it up and looks at it. She takes a bite

James Anderson rushes in

James That bloke must be a real nut case.
Vicky What the hell do you mean?
James Well, first he was only wearing one shoe and second, he's just put two pounds in the Barnardo's box.
Vicky That was payment for the books. He's a charming man, he asked me to have dinner with him.
James Some people have the cheek of the devil—you're not going to?
Vicky Yes, of course I am. Do me good to get out.
James Oh.
Vicky Why are you looking at me like that?
James I got a large chicken for tonight, what shall I do with it?
Vicky I don't know. Why don't you stuff it? Come on, let's do some work.

Vicky exits to the shop munching her apple

CURTAIN

SCENE 2

The same. That evening

When the CURTAIN *rises, James, in a butcher's apron, is pottering about in the kitchen. The shop bell jangles, and Henry enters*

Henry I'm back. You can all come out of your cupboards and live a little. (*He goes to the kitchen*) Good evening, James Anderson, what a delicious smell, can it be you?
James It's the dinner, it's in the oven.

Henry You are clever. What is it, a simple haggis *à la Provençale* or something exotic?
James It's *Poulet en Cocotte Bonne Femme.*

James bangs the cutlery and plates down

Henry I love the way you say that like Edith Piaf singing "I Belong to Glasgow". Cook is surly tonight. Been at the gin again, have we?

Henry sits in the armchair

James How was your driving lesson?
Henry Dreary, not a single near miss. I think he drove all the time on those sneaky dual controls. And the mean sod refused to let me give a lift to a hitch-hiking sailor; wouldn't you say that was unpatriotic?

James puts the bread basket on the table. He gets on preparing the meal. Henry opens his evening paper and races through it

Henry I don't know why I buy the paper on Saturdays, it's full of football results—(*he twists the paper round*)—and footballers. I wonder if I'm too old to train as a masseur?
James Masseur. Why do you want to be a masseur?

Henry raises his eyes briefly to heaven. He goes back to examining the paper

Henry Yes, it might be worth making inquiries at the local polytechnic. I've often been told I had a nice touch.
James You'd lose your Civil Service pension.
Henry But I'd die with a smile on my face.
James You do have some foolish notions.
Henry I'm not the only one—you finished writing that novel of yours yet?
James Aye, it's being typed.
Henry I can't wait to read it. Am I in it?
James No it's on a serious theme.
Henry Oh, repartee, I think you're making a big mistake, sounds to me as if it could do with pepping up a bit. Go on, write me in.
James You would not fit in. My story's set in the Highlands.
Henry The mind boggles. How's Vicky, is she glittering as much as you?
James She's all right.
Henry Why only two places? The poor creature's got to eat something, be it only the parson's nose.
James She's been invited out to dinner.
Henry What! Don't you believe it.
James It's true. She hasn't stopped mentioning it all afternoon.
Henry The clever cunning cow.
James What do you mean?
Henry Well, it's obvious. She wouldn't dare sit here in the fat dress and make a pig of herself, so she's decided to cheat. One last glorious tour round all the chip shops stuffing herself silly, I bet.
James I don't think so.

Henry I know her better than you do. It's like living with an alcoholic, junky, kleptomaniac. You wait, these next few weeks are going to be murder. She'll announce some grand new diet and beg us both to help her and then she'll be up to every trick in the book. She'll sit here large as—larger than life, moaning away and nibbling a carrot and all the time there'll be cream cakes behind the cistern and Mars bars up her knickers. I know our Vicky.

James goes to the living area, takes a cigarette and lights it

James I saw the man.
Henry Man? What man? Where?
James The one she's going out with. He only had one shoe.
Henry Oh. How many feet?
James Two.
Henry You counted?
James Very brown.
Henry A nig nog?
James With fair hair.
Henry Dyed or natural?
James Aye, it's unnatural.
Henry My dear boy, what are you smoking?
James And she wanted me to cut his toe-nails.
Henry Pull yourself together, James Anderson. Are you trying to tell me that our little Vicky's got a date with a one-legged, peroxided, spade with ingrowing toe-nails?
James Why do you have to make a joke out of everything? The chap was quite good looking.

James goes into the dining area

Henry With that lot, he'd have to be. Who is he?
James He came to buy a book, I don't know who he is.
Henry Does she?
James I didn't ask her. After all, it's none of my business.
Henry Oh, you're hopeless. You'll get no joy out of life with that attitude. Fancy. Madame going out to dinner—shouldn't think she's had a date since VJ Day.
James What's VJ day?
Henry What a vicious thing to say. There's a very mean streak in you, I hope and pray that some day someone asks you what the Common Market was.
James I don't know what you're talking about.
Henry That's what I'm complaining about, you tartan twit.
James You'll have to ask Vicky yourself.
Henry Ask her what?
James Who this man is she's going out with.

James goes to the kitchen and takes off his apron

Henry Oh, that? Don't worry, I will. Lay the thumbscrews casually on the table. What's she doing, slipping into something tight? Vicky?

Vicky? There's a police officer here wants to book you for obstruction. (*He shouts up the stairs*) Vicky?

Vicky (*off*) I won't be a minute. I'm in the bathroom.

Henry What, again? You're going to turn into Moby Dick if you keep this up. Had a good look at your feet lately? Using a mirror, of course.

Vicky Shut up, and pour me a drink.

Henry She wants a drink. (*He moves towards the drinks table*)

Henry Do you want a drink, James?

James No, thanks, I'm going out to get some cigarettes. (*He moves towards the door*)

Henry There's a packet on the table, unless Vicky's filled it with chocolate ones—no, you've got one on.

James I don't like those. I won't be long.

James exits quickly

Henry shrugs and pours two drinks, one huge, one minute

Henry Drink to me only with thy thighs and . . .

The shop bell jangles

Vicky comes out of the bathroom wearing a long loose caftan and carrying a nail file

Vicky Have a nice day at the office, dear? (*She files her nails*)

Henry As a matter of fact—(*he turns and sees her and begins to walk around her with a drink in each hand*)—the typists' pool voted me the male they would most like to be trapped in the lift with.

Vicky You'd better use the stairs in future then, hadn't you?

Henry Clever, devilishly clever.

Vicky Just an idle quip.

Henry I mean that caftan thing, it wins hands down over the fat dress.

Vicky I got it this afternoon. You really like?

Henry Sensational, very Arabian Nights. We'll have to call you Fatima.

Vicky I don't look like a tent? (*She stretches out both arms*)

Henry Definitely not. A marquee or even a tall traffic bollard, but not a tent, no. I can't visualize a couple of Boy Scouts frying sausages outside your flap.

Vicky It's nice to be reassured.

Henry pecks her on the cheek

Henry You look super, absolutely super. I've never seen you look better. Cheers, love.

He hands her the minute drink, Vicky stares at it

Vicky I wouldn't have believed it possible to pour a drink that didn't cover the bottom of a glass.

Henry It's a very large bottom.

Vicky firmly grabs his drink and pours part of it into her glass

Vicky That's better. Cheers.

Henry You're being reckless and foolish.

Vicky I'm having a last fling. (*She sits on the sofa*) Tomorrow I'm starting a new diet and you've all got to help me 'cause you know what I'm like.

Henry I don't know if I can go through with it all again. Tying your wrists to the bedposts every night and binding up your mouth with Sellotape. Maybe your new friend will co-operate.

Vicky What new friend?

Henry This mysterious stranger you're going out with.

Vicky Oh, him.

Henry Yes, oh him.

Vicky Who told you about it?

Henry Blabbermouth Anderson. Who is he?

Vicky None of your business, Henry dear. I don't quiz you about your gentlemen callers, unless they steal the silver.

Henry God, you're not still going on about that teapot?

Vicky It was rather valuable.

Henry Yes, a collector's item—Sheffield plate made in Yokohama, very sought after.

Vicky It belonged to my grandmother.

Henry (*sitting in the armchair*) Your grandmother was a fool and stop changing the subject, what's this man's name?

Vicky I can't remember.

Henry You're beginning to sound like me.

Vicky I do hope not. Anything but that. Why this sudden and ridiculous interest in whom I'm going out with, anyway.

Henry I've always been fascinated by the unusual and bizarre, so come on, be a sport. Let me have my vicarious thrills and tell me what you're up to.

Vicky There's nothing to it, he's just a customer.

Henry I see. (*Rising*) Pure chance that you've bought a new frock, washed your hair and heaven knows what else?

Vicky Yes.

Henry White-haired old gent, is he—with a stick and roving hands? Naughty girl, pinch your botty, pinch your botty? (*He sits on the sofa beside Vicky*)

Vicky He's a lot younger than you.

Henry That tells me nothing, I happen to be very well preserved.

Vicky He doesn't have your pickled look. He's rather delightful and quite dishy in a butch sort of way, and that's all I'm prepared to say.

Henry No matter. I'll read all the rest in the *News of the World*.

Vicky What do you mean?

Henry Wait a sec. I'll have one of my psychic turns. "Police are looking for a rather delightful, dishy, butch gentleman who in the early hours of this morning flung the buxom body of Victoria Hope on to the Heath from a passing car."

Vicky Stop, you're being horrid. You're going to ruin my evening.

Henry rises

Henry "When interviewed her stunningly beautiful lodger, Henry Simmonds, dabbed his luscious almond-shaped eyes with a black chiffon
hanky and stated that he had repeatedly warned the silly cow about
casual pick-ups but . . ."

Vicky That's your life story, not mine.

Henry I happen to be an excellent judge of character.

Vicky And I'm not, I suppose?

Henry You don't have my experience.

Vicky That's something to be grateful for.

Henry And in what dark alley have you arranged to meet this total
stranger?

Vicky He's picking me up—he's calling for me here.

Vicky gets another drink

Henry What a bit of luck! I'll be able to do an excellent identi-kit picture
of him. They'd never find him from James Anderson's description, so
ordinary.

Vicky I gave him some books. He's taking me out to show his gratitude.
And that's all there is to it. Perfectly staightforward, so will you please
change the subject. (*She sits in the armchair*)

Henry Just as you like. What have you left me in your will?

Vicky All my clothes.

Henry How divine. Your fur coat will make a lovely bedspread and there
should be enough left over for matching curtains. (*He pours another
drink*)

Vicky Oh, you are a mean sod. I'm going to be on tenterhooks the whole
evening now. Every tiny move he makes I shall expect to be strangled.

Henry Vicky, Vicky, you really must stop jumping to conclusions. He
may after all be a comparatively harmless rapist.

Vicky Oh, thank you, that'll be nice. Something to look forward to.

Henry Best to be prepared—these things happen.

Vicky Not to sweet little girls like me, they don't.

The doorbell rings

Aah! My God, that's him.

Henry (*in a harsh whisper*) Shall we turn all the lights out and pretend to
be asleep)

Vicky Stop being silly. Go and let him in. And for Christ's sake, try and
behave normally.

Henry You do ask a lot of me.

Henry makes the sign of the cross and exits

Vicky moves to the dining area. The shop bell rings

Henry (*off*) Aah! No, no. I swear to you, she's not in. No. Gone to visit her granny in Brixton. Please, please I beg you, put that whopping chopper down.

Henry backs into the room with his hands up

Now, don't do anything hasty. People like you need help. Let's talk this over. (*Aside to Vicky*) Hide under the sofa quick.

Vicky is paralysed, staring at the door with her mouth open in amazement. Henry gets down on his knees

I got a wife and four kids, mister.

Slowly, a puzzled James Anderson enters

Henry rolls back on to the floor, laughing

Vicky Pitiful. Absolutely pitiful. (*She sits on the sofa*)
Henry Ha, ha, ha. Admit you weren't quite sure, go on admit it.
Vicky You didn't fool me for a second, I was just horrified at what the poor man must be thinking. (*To James*) And what did you want to go and ring the doorbell for, you idiot?
James I'm sorry, I forgot my key. What's going on?
Vicky Henry, what else?
Henry We're waiting. It's going to be like *The Heiress* all over again— Olivia de Havilland listening for the horse-drawn carriage, rushing to the window, better get that oil lamp lit for the final scene.
Vicky Do give over. Is there any ice, James Anderson?
James Yes. I'll get some. You look very smart, Vicky.
Henry She's had a puncture, I've rung the A.A.

James goes to the kitchen. Henry begins to laugh again

Vicky Stupid clot. What's the time?
Henry Two minutes past seven—let's face it, you've been stood up.
Vicky Oh, why didn't I arrange to meet him outside Swan and Edgar's?
James The chicken will be done in ten minutes.
Henry So will Vicky.
Vicky Belt up.
Henry I'm sorry, I do apologize. I've got over-excited like an anxious father at his baby's first date.

Vicky rolls her eyes to heaven

What do you think he's really after?
Vicky My money I should think, wouldn't you?
Henry Could be.
Vicky Oh, don't be so ridiculous.
Henry He might be a beginner—you can't expect him to kick off with Barbara Hutton.

Henry sits on the sofa. James returns with ice

James Who wants ice?

Vicky holds out her glass

Vicky I do and some drink to go with it, please.

James takes her glass and goes to the drinks table

Henry Is he Italian by any chance?
Vicky No, why?
Henry Remember Venice?
Vicky Venice?
Henry The Piazza San Marco, you got your bum pinched by twenty-seven men, simultaneously. They like a bit of flesh, the Ities, and what about that gondolier that chased you up the canals shouting, "*Che bella, che fatso*", or whatever the Italian is?
Vicky He was horrid.
Henry He was a steaming great dish.
Vicky (*smiling*) Yes, you did get a bit lemon-lipped about that.
Henry I even wore several bulky sweaters the following evening and all I got was hot.

James brings Vicky her whisky

Vicky Thank you.
James There's plenty of food for three if your fellow doesn't turn up, Vicky.
Vicky And thank you too, James Anderson.
James Oh, I'm sorry—I didn't mean to—that is, I'm . . .
Henry Inarticulate. We know, there's no need to press the point. Go and and poke that chicken about or something.

James drifts morosely to the kitchen

Vicky What time is it?
Henry Never mind the time. Now, this man, did you say his name was Christie? Crippen?
Vicky He's an Englishman by the name of Tom Reynolds. He is a geologist who works for an oil company. He is of average height and weight, well mannered, pleasant and polite *and* normal—one hundred per cent.
Henry What are you doing? Compiling a dossier on him? Relax, I'll get at the truth with a few well-chosen, subtle questions.

The doorbell rings. One ring. Da, di di di di—dum dum

How common. I'll get it, always willing to sacrifice myself for my friends.

Vicky pushes him back in his seat

Vicky Stay where you are, we don't want to risk a repeat performance. James Anderson, be an angel and let my guest in, please.
James Sure, Vicky.

Henry (*in a loud whisper*) Pssst. Don't look into his eyes. It could prove fatal.

James What?

Vicky Pay no attention, go and answer the door.

James exits

Vicky anxiously looks for something behind the sofa

Henry Now, are you sure you've got everything? Pepper, hatpin, police whistle, crucifix, silver bullet? Why are you all of a twitch?

Vicky Shut up, I can't find my bloody handbag.

Henry Don't get in a flap, I'm sitting on it. Here you are, all lovely and warm.

He hands the bag to her. She goes to him

Vicky Thank you and if you start camping around in front of him, I'll have your guts for garters.

Henry When have I ever let you down? (*Rising*) Oh, quick turn round, what a good job I noticed.

Vicky turns in a panic

Vicky What is it? What is it?

Henry tugs at her dress

Henry There's a cushion—oh, no, it is your arse.

Vicky swipes him on the side of his head with her handbag

Tom and James come in and stand by the door

Ow! That hurt, you bloody bitch. (*He sees Tom and James and stands up, hitches his trousers, and extends a hand*) How do? Cum in, cum right in, lad. Make theeself at 'ome.

Tom Good evening. I found the bell all right.

Vicky Yes, so I heard.

Tom You're looking marvellous.

Henry Aye, she's a striking lass, our Vicky. She is that an' all.

Vicky Come in and meet everybody. That's James Anderson who let you in.

Tom Happy to meet you. Tom Reynolds.

Tom and James shake hands

James How do you do?

Vicky And this is Henry Simmonds—I wouldn't get too close to him, he sounds as if he's sickening for something.

Henry Champion to meet, Tom lad, champion.

Tom Hello, Henry.

Tom and Henry shake hands

Henry Eeeee! Don't thee have enormous hands, Tom lad?
Tom Have I?
Henry Aye, proper whoppers—why thee could break a horse's neck with
hands that size.
Tom I can't imagine that I'd want to.
Vicky I should think not indeed. What a silly thing to say, Henry, and
what a silly voice to say it in. I'm sorry, Tom, he's always acting the
fool, it's best to ignore him. Sit down, please.

Vicky pulls one arm, Henry the other. Henry wins. Tom sits in the armchair

Tom Thank you.
Henry Why don't thee pull your young man a pint of Bass, our Vicky?
Vicky (*snapping*) Isn't it time you took the whippet out for a slash,
Grandad?
Henry (*dropping his accent*) I beg your pardon. Do remember we have a
guest, Victoria.
Vicky I'm sorry, what would you like to drink, Tom? We've got gin,
whisky, vodka, sherry.
Tom Vodka, please.
Vicky Anything with it?
Tom Just ice, if there is some.

Vicky pours a drink. Henry and James stare at Tom. Tom smiles

Tom I didn't expect to meet such a crowd.
Henry Did you hear that, Vicky? Tom thought you lived alone.
Vicky There are times when I wish I did.

Henry stands still and smiles

Tom I like these houses on the hill.
Henry They are nice and they're worth a bomb now. Vicky owns this
one, you know, freehold.
Tom Lucky girl.

Vicky returns with a drink for Tom and sits

Vicky I hope that's all right.
Tom Fine, thanks. Skol.
Henry Bottoms up.
Tom Are the three of you related in any way?
Vicky Heaven forbid. No, we're just good friends.
Henry He's bound to find out. Why not tell him the truth—Mummy?

Henry sits on the sofa

Vicky They are also my lodgers and liable to be flung on to the streets
at a moment's notice. A fact that they tend to forget at times.

James gets a drink and sits

Henry She's power mad.
Tom It's never been my luck to have a landlady as charming as you.

Henry Don't you believe it, she's absolutely dreadful—notes everywhere. "Kindly leave this bed as you would wish to find it", "No naked visitors allowed after eleven", "Don't eat this strand of spaghetti, it's mine". I tell you, life here can be a nightmare.

Vicky Henry likes to exaggerate.

Tom I had gathered that. (*To Henry*) Are you on the stage?

Henry Quite a lot of the time metaphorically speaking, but I actually work in an office.

Tom Interesting.

Henry Not very, I'm a Civil Servant.

Vicky You'd never believe it, would you?

Henry I'm in New Scotland Yard, work very closely with Interpol tracing international rapists and confidence men.

Tom Sounds like very worthwhile work.

Henry Yes, I'm dedicated, they never get away. I was made Honorary Colonel of the Canadian Mounties, for obvious reasons.

Vicky Don't listen to a word, Tom. He's a tax inspector, in the Finchley Road.

Henry I've told you never to tell people that, they go off me. Look at poor Tom, his eyes are hooded with guilt already.

Tom No, you're mistaken, I'm very law abiding, pay all my taxes, my TV licence and declare everything at the Customs.

Henry What do you do for excitement?

Tom Ha, well—er, I read a lot.

Vicky James Anderson here is a budding author. He's just finished his first novel. He also helps me in the bookshop—runs it, really, runs the whole house in fact, don't you, James? James?

James Pardon?

Henry Thank God for that—I thought somebody had cut his vocal chords.

James What line of business might you be in, Mr Reynolds?

Tom I work for an oil company.

Vicky He's flying off to Persia in the morning.

Henry Plane or carpet?

Tom I don't think I'd notice, it's a six am flight.

James Are you permanently based in Persia, then?

Tom No, I go where the work is, Libya, Burma, Borneo, North Wales.

James Doing what?

Tom Scouting out new territories for possible oilfields—prospecting, really, in a scientific way.

Henry How fascinating! Tell me, do you keep being covered with black oil and Susan Hayward?

Tom Ha, 'fraid not. It's not as exciting as they make it out to be in the movies.

Henry You astonish me—I always found the films pretty dreary.

Vicky Henry finds most things "pretty dreary".

James Who's Susan Hayward?

Henry You will get your vocal chords cut.

Vicky I don't suppose you go to the pictures much?

Tom I do, a fair amount. Mind you, it's sometimes a little confusing, I saw *The Boy Friend* in Cairo, dubbed in French and with Arabic subtitles.

Henry That must have been an improvement. What did you think of Twiggy?

Tom Charming and delightful.

Henry That's interesting. Do you like Mia Farrow?

Tom Yes, she's sensational.

Henry Vicky hates Mia Farrow.

Vicky I wouldn't say that.

Henry All right, detests her then. The plot thickens, you obviously don't have any Italian blood.

Tom I don't quite follow?

Vicky It's best not to where Henry's concerned. Does your wife travel with you?

Tom No, I'm not married.

Henry I can't believe it. What an incredible coincidence, neither am I.

Tom I'm afraid I don't quite see the connection.

Vicky There would only be one if you were both bachelors for the same reason, and that's ridiculous.

Henry Is it?

Vicky Yes, you can't both have had it shot off at the Battle of the Somme.

Henry I told you that in confidence, Vicky, you promised you'd never tell.

Henry gets up and goes to get another drink. James rises and goes to the kitchen

James Excuse me, I want to check the oven.

Vicky James Anderson is a marvellous cook, we're thoroughly spoiled.

Tom I hope you approve of my choise of restaurant then. Do you like Italian food?

Vicky I adore it.

Henry And it adores her, clings to her, you might say.

Tom If you're ready I think we should go, I booked for seven-thirty.

Vicky Always ready to eat—story of my life.

Vicky and Tom rise

Henry Sure you won't have another drink, Thomas?

Tom No, thanks. Nice meeting you, Henry. See you at Xmas I hope.

Henry Xmas? Oh—yes, why not. Bring back a Bedouin for my stocking.

Tom Do my best. Good-bye, Jimmy, good luck with the writing.

James Yes. Good-bye.

Henry Don't forget there's a full moon tonight, Vicky.

Vicky How romantic.

Henry Do you want me to wait up for you, just in case?

Vicky I think I've seen enough of you for today. 'Bye.

Tom I hope we're going to be very late. As it's my last night in the old

country for a while, I'd like to really celebrate if that's all right with you, Vicky?
Vicky Why not? Sunday tomorrow. Come on. Be good you two.

Tom and Vicky exit

Henry (*shouting*) I won't contact the missing person's bureau till the morning. (*He wanders towards the kitchen*) What did you think of him?
James He's all right, I suppose. I didn't like him much, though.
Henry Mmm. A bit too dull to be true. I wonder if she hired him?
James What do you mean?
Henry From an escort agency, Rent-a-Fella, or something like that.
James Why would she waste her money?
Henry To give her sagging ego a lift.
Henry But he was here this morning looking at books.
Henry You're right, it's too elaborate and Vicky's not that good an actress. Did you notice the blatant banality of, "Is your wife travelling with you?". I thought she was joking but no, her face was glowing like an honest pudding.
James Did you notice he didn't say which oil company he worked for?
Henry That's true, he's probably just the paraffin man covered in mantan. On the other hand he did have that ten year out-of-date vocabulary that expatriates seem to cling to.
James He seemed genuinely taken with her.
Henry Lust or cannibalism?
James You don't have to be disgusting.
Henry Well, he has been in some funny foreign parts, could have picked up some funny foreign ways. I mean to say, North Wales, anything can happen there. And Borneo—Borneo—that's it. I've got it, James Anderson, he's a body shrinker. And of course it would be a challenge. Poor Vicky, if there's a large dried apricot on the doorstep in the morning, don't cook it, give it a decent Christian burial.

Jame sits at the dining-table with a book. Henry goes to him

Where's this *Poule en Cocotte* whatsisname?
James It will be a few minutes yet. (*He reads his book*)
Henry Poetry in motion. (*He sits*)
James What?
Henry The way you turned that page. Sheer poetry. Nureyev couldn't have done it better. (*Pause*) You should get a job in Madame Tussaud's you could be the attendant that makes everyone jump.

James goes as if to speak

Aah! He moved, Mummy, he moved and I've wet my knickers . . .

James goes back to reading

You really are a sad creature. It's pathetic the way you cling to this little womb every evening. Eighteen and hiding in books—leading other people's lives. If you want to opt out you ought to do it with style. You'd hardly credit it but I found you quite intriguing when you first arrived. Funny how shallow people can often appear interesting—one convinces oneself that they are hiding something, I suppose . . .

James turns a page. Henry stands behind James's chair. James turns another page

What would happen if I were to approach you? To touch you in some secret place? Does the thought tighten your bladder, Wee Jimmy Anderson? Does it? Would you shrivel or explode? Wither or flower?

James turns another page

You don't read that fast, James. Rest it on your knees, your hands are trembling almost imperceptibly like humming-bird wings. With manly rage, I'm sure. (*He smiles and straightens up and circles the chair*) What would it be, I wonder? A woodland plant with tiny, colourless petals? A sturdy, prickly thistle? Or would you surprise us all—a huge, exotic desert bloom, the kind that only reveals itself once in twenty years, but is well worth waiting for? Eh? Ha, ha, ha. Shall I pollinate you, James Anderson? Shall I? Bzzz, bzzz bzzz. Watch out, petal face, here I come. (*He swerves and bends nearer*) Bzz. Buzz. Buzz.

James closes his book and looks up. Henry bends over him and brings his face close to James. They gaze silently at each other for a second, then Henry smiles and touches James on the nose with a finger-tip

Buzz.

The kitchen pinger sounds. Henry sits and pours himself some wine. James gets the casserole out of the oven, angrily slamming the oven door. He places the casserole on the table, removes the lid, and sits

Henry I say that looks almost as lovely as you do. Isn't it nice just the two of us, shall I light the candles to make it more cosy and romantic?

James I like to see what I'm eating; and while we're about it, Henry, I'd be grateful if you'd refrain from these constant effeminate allusions that I find both embarrassing and inaccurate.

Henry My, my, everyone's very sharp tonight. Must be some kind of virus around. I do hope I don't catch it. But seriously, James Anderson, you must realize that it's almost a disease, part of my condition, a brave shallow mask. However, if I have truly given offence, I apologize and I give you my solemn promise that nothing of a similar nature will occur again.

James That's all right. Do you want some bread?

Henry Thank you. You are good to me, Moira.

CURTAIN

SCENE 3

The same. The following morning

The church bells are ringing softly. James is sitting on the sofa with a cup of coffee and a weekly review supplement. He looks at his watch. Henry comes slowly down the stairs

Henry Oh, hello. Love locked in? What time is it?

James Half-past twelve.

Henry Is it really? (*He yawns*) Oooah, my face is going to take at least three hours to settle.

James It's a cold lunch today.

Henry Lunch? Lunch, what's that? I'm looking for coffee.

James In the pot, I just made some more.

Henry pours out some coffee in the kitchen, then moves towards the dining-table, picking up a Sunday paper off the table as he goes

Henry Oh good, it's Sunday.

The bells stop

What's that poofy Jilly Cooper got to say for herself this week? (*He pours himself a cup of coffee*) How's Vicky? Recovered from her night out?

James She's not back yet.

Henry Oh. What did you say?

James I said she's not back yet.

Henry Not back, she's never been out all night, ever.

James She came back last night, I heard them.

Henry Them? Tom as well?

James Yes.

Henry James Anderson, you're blushing, as pretty as a sunset over the heather—what did you hear?

James Nothing—voices. Just voices.

Henry goes into the living area

Henry You bloody liar, you saw them, didn't you?

James No, I came down for my book, they were here in the dark on the sofa.

Henry So she actually managed to pull him, did she? Good for her and what bliss for us she'll be in a good mood for a couple of months. Where is she now?

James I don't know. They both left in a taxi about four-thirty in the morning.

Henry You've obviously had a very good night's sleep. Four-thirty! Of course he had an early flight to catch. Mystery solved, nothing to worry about—except this. (*He picks up a pink fluffy animal*) It's evil, absolutely evil, what is it? Makes the room look like a tart's bedroom.

James It was here when I got up, I think it must be Vicky's.

Henry You're right, it's the sort of thing she'd get lumbered with. Other girls get diamond bracelets, our Vicky gets souvenirs. Stop looking so glum. (*He throws the fluffy toy to James*)

James That chap's plane was supposed to leave at six, it's now gone half-past twelve. Could she have gone with him?

Henry Of course not. Cost him a fortune, all that excess weight.

The doorbell rings

There you are, safely back in one large piece.

James It can't be Vicky. She's got her key, I checked.

Henry We have been a busy bee. Well, go on, answer it.

James moves to the door

Or if by some happy chance it's a couple of those clean-cut Mormon gentlemen, send them in to convert me.

James exits. The shop bell jangles

Henry goes to pour himself another cup of coffee, singing to himself, at the dining-table. He sits

James arrives with a large bunch of gift-wrapped flowers

Who was it?

James Flowers for Vicky.

Henry At least it's not a wreath. Who are they from?

James There's a card.

Henry What does it say?

James It's sealed.

Henry Well, open it.

James I couldn't do that—it's against my principles.

Henry How middle class can you get? Give it to me. (*He takes it*) I don't understand you, you spend the whole night behaving like a cross between Agatha Christie and a traffic warden, yet you baulk at opening a tiny envelope.

James That's something private.

Henry If the Inter-Flora girl can read it, so can I. They always use very cheap glue on these dolly things. If you get your nail under in the right place—it comes away—without a trace—whoops. (*The envelope tears*)

James You'll never get it together again.

Henry We'll say it got caught in the letter-box.

James You don't push flowers through a letter-box.

Henry Ssssh, this is the interesting bit. It's from Tom. Oooooh!

James What does he say?

Henry Sure you want to know? Makes you an accessory.

James Tell me.

Henry (*reading the card*) "Can't get you out of my mind." How did she

manage to get in, he must have ears like Dumbo. "All my love, Tom."
Aaaah.

James At least we know she hasn't left the country.

The shop doorbell jangles

Henry Quick, that must be her, swallow the envelope.

He shoves the tiny envelope at James, who runs towards the kitchen. Henry pops the note on the flowers on the chest of drawers and throws himself into a chair

Vicky enters slowly and dreamily

Vicky Hello, Henry. James.

Henry What happened? Didn't you fetch your reserve price?

Vicky What? No. Tom's flight was delayed. We had several breakfasts at the airport and then we—we just sat and chatted. He is nice, terribly nice. (*She picks up the toy animal and sits on the sofa with it on her lap*)

James Lunch won't be long, Vicky.

Vicky Good. Can I help? What are you cocking—cooking?

Henry We heard you the first time, dear. What a personal remark. So that's the sort of thing you go round saying. "Oh yes, James Anderson does all the cocking in our house, he's so good at it, Henry and I thrive on it."

Vicky It was a slip of the tongue.

Henry Slip! It was an avalanche. Mind you it would make very good television, sure to top the ratings. We present James Anderson, The Galloping Cock.

Vicky I'm sorry, James Anderson, we're obviously going to be plagued with this sort of rubbish for weeks. (*She rises*)

James Don't worry, Vicky, I don't mind.

Henry I should think not, all that wonderful free advertising.

Vicky sees the flowers

Vicky What gorgeous flowers, are they for me? (*She reads the card*)

Henry Yes, they just arrived.

James prepares salad and cold meats in the kitchen

Vicky The darling, how sweet. They're from Tom.

Henry Are they? James said they were, I don't know how he knew.

Vicky I must put them in water, they're beautiful.

Henry takes them from her and hands them to James in the kitchen

Henry That's James Anderson's department. You sit down and tell me about your evening. I can't wait to hear. Would that little pink thing like to go in water, too, it might improve it.

Vicky sits at the table

Vicky Don't you dare. It has immense sentimental value.

Henry Pity. Now, I'm all ears.

Henry sits at the table

Vicky I don't know where to begin, it was all perfect. Tom is terribly funny when you get to know him. We went to a marvellous restaurant where I tried to be good but eventually made an incredible pig of myself. The sweet trolley alone was paradise.

Henry Natch.

Vicky Then something happened that you'll never believe.

Henry Try me.

Vicky He took me to a nightclub. Honestly. No, you'd have adored it. There was this smashing bird that did the most impossible things with her tits.

Henry Really? What she do, stuff them in her ears?

Vicky No, you fool. She had tassels and they rotated—at speed and in different directions.

Henry What, that old trick? Sarah Bernhardt used to do it.

Vicky Well, I'd never seen it.

Henry And I hope you don't try it or you'll knock all the pictures off the wall.

Vicky I also danced for the first time in years and I was rather good, what's more.

Henry You must take it up professionally, it should only take us about a year to sew the sequins on. Anyway, let's skip all that and get to the interesting bit. What happened when you got back here?

Vicky Why—er—we had a few drinks and chatted till it was time to go to the airport.

Henry You sat and chatted?

Vicky Yes.

James begins to mix the salad dressing noisily. Henry looks at him and he runs to a stop. Henry looks back at Vicky

Henry That's not what I was told. High jinks, I heard. James Anderson blushed.

James I didn't—I—it was accidental.

Pause

Vicky (*quietly*) Oh, you bastards. You bloody, bloody bastards. (*She begins to weep*)

Henry is appalled and quickly kneels and grabs her hands

Henry Darling, please, it was only a shot in the dark. Nothing happened. James Anderson's not the Peeping Tom type and I was flat out, as usual. I'm sorry, deeply sorry, it was a foul trick to play on you. I'll never do it again I promise, I didn't realize it was important. Please forgive me.

Vicky pulls herself together

Vicky It's all right, you swine, I might have guessed. I didn't mind you knowing—it was—it was just the thought that all the time . . .

Henry I know, horrid, nasty.

Vicky Don't suppose it's important, anyway. Ships that pass in the night and all that jazz.

Henry Why don't you do something about it?

Vicky How can I? He's miles away. He is coming back in four months, in time for Christmas and he has promised to write but he probably won't.

Henry He already has, you got that little card, didn't you?

Vicky That's true.

Henry Well then.

Vicky kisses Henry on the cheek and they lean against each other holding hands

James Anybody object to tarragon with the salad? (*He gets no answer so begins to shred it into the salad bowl*)

Henry Christmas—four months—yes, you could do it.

Vicky Do what?

Henry Show yourself off to your best advantage. Go on a proper diet and stick to it for a change.

Vicky Wouldn't do much good, my glands are wrong.

Henry It's me you're talking to. I've seen the family album—little Vicky showing her bum on a rug, little Vicky in her first camp party dress. Little Vicky doesn't become Big Bertha till she's about sixteen.

Vicky They said it was puppy fat, the liars.

Henry Then Vicky seems to vanish from the album. The odd glimpse of a blob behind two or three uncles and aunts, nothing more.

Vicky I've always hated having my photograph taken.

Henry With reason. But you've got super legs and very tiny hands, it's only in between that you're king size.

Vicky I could do with losing a few pounds.

Henry You could do with losing a few hundred. How much do you weigh?

Vicky I don't know I never weigh myself.

Henry My guess is about thirteen stone, give or take fourteen pounds.

Vicky I've never been more than eleven-and-a-half in my life.

Henry How do you know if you never weigh yourself? Eleven-and-a-half —I've got news for you.

Vicky (*moving away to the sofa*) Henry, I don't want to argue, I'm feeling happy.

Henry You could be a lot happier. You could be wearing a size twelve dress when Prince Charming returns and hear him cry, "It fits, it fits", before he rips it off.

Vicky Tom likes me for myself. (*She sits on the sofa*)

Henry He hardly knows you.

Vicky We get on terribly well and he doesn't care what I wear.

Henry In that case I apologize. Go ahead, wear dungarees and a paper bag over your head, your exceptional personality is bound to shine through and captivate millions.

Pause

Vicky I think it's sad that appearances count that much with you.
Henry In the long run they don't. But initially about ninety per cent.
Vicky I looked much the same when you first met me six or seven years ago.
Henry You looked far worse six years ago, you had spots.
Vicky And yet we became friends, good friends.
Henry I'm a special case, luv. To be honest, I thought you looked a nice safe girl who wouldn't expect me to take her home and ravish her.
Vicky How right you were.

Pause

Henry And you did have a deliciously dirty laugh.
Vicky And I was very naive, I thought you were just artistic.

Henry laughs

Henry So what about this rigid diet? They say that inside every fat girl there's a thin one trying to get out.
Vicky I'm different. Inside me there's an even fatter girl waiting to charge out—and one day I think she's going to make it.
Henry There's got to be a limit. Skin can't stretch that far.
Vicky I still think you're wrong, about people I mean and what they react to.
Henry Vicky darling, millions are spent every year on advertising and packaging, surely you can spend four months redesigning yourself, especially with such a good reason?
Vicky Maybe.

James comes to the edge of the living area

James Lunch is on the table.
Henry What a nice change from it being on the floor.

Vicky rises

Vicky I don't know, I'll think about it, I'm still not convinced.

Vicky exits to the bathroom

Henry rushes to the chest of drawers and opens it

Henry James Anderson, come here at once.
James What's the matter?
Henry We've got to help Vicky. To strike while the iron is hot. Where are the bloody things. Ah, yes, these are them. (*He pulls out some dusters and cleaning things, then a pair of very large beach pyjama bottoms*)
James What are they?
Henry Beach pyjamas, long before your time. She had them specially made for our holiday in Ibiza but she never got drunk enough to wear them. Hurry up, get into them.

James But what will . . .

Henry Don't argue. If you love Vicky, do it. It's for her good. Red alert, no time for questions.

James gets into the bottoms. Henry drags out the matching top and puts his arm through one sleeve

No, no, you fool, just get into one leg, where do you think I'm going to go?

James You mean we're both going to wear it?

Henry At last. Go to the top of the class.

Henry gets into one pyjama leg, bullies James into the other and pulls the trousers up (elastic waist)

James Vicky will go mad.

Henry No, she won't. She's got a lovely sense of humour. Get your arm in and watch where you put your other hand.

They get the top round them and Henry manages to do up one button

Stop that sexy wriggle or you'll regret it.

They jump round and shuffle a bit

Isn't it cosy, we must do this more often. Don't forget, look casual.

Vicky comes out of the bathroom, down the stairs and into the room. She stops dead when she sees them

Vicky What's this?

Henry Shock treatment.

Vicky goes to the sofa, sits, picks up the cigarette packet. She tries to smile

Vicky Well—well, it's—it's bloody well worked.

Vicky bursts into tears and runs upstairs, sobbing, as—

the CURTAIN *falls*

ACT II

SCENE 1

The same. Four months later

There is a streamer on the back wall saying, "Lose a Ton for Tom", and a graph with a declining line. Some Christmas cards have been put up, and there is snow on the window. There is a portable electric sauna on the floor, covered with a sheet

James is discovered at the stove watching a pan and listening to music on the radio. The telephone rings. James starts to go to it, returns to take the pan off the stove, returns again and switches off the radio. Finally he runs to the telephone and picks up the receiver

James Hello? . . . Oh, hello, Barry, how was New York? . . . No luck so far. I've collected a lot of rejection slips . . . Aye, it's difficult with a first novel . . . Henry's not in at the moment . . . same as usual. He should be in any minute, he's gone for a run on the Heath . . . No, nothing like that, Vicky does the running, Henry cycles and shouts at her through a megaphone . . . Aye, it is. All right, I'll tell him. 'Bye.

James returns to the kitchen and switches on the radio. The shop bell jangles. James begins to pour hot soup into a mug

Henry staggers in, shivering in an overcoat, long woollen scarf and gloves. Hears the music, and does a little dance

Henry Oh, that's nice. This is going to be the death of me. It's freezing, absolutely freezing. I'm moving but I can't feel anything. Total anaesthesia.

James switches off the radio

James Barry's back from America, he just telephoned.
Henry Big deal! The way I feel I don't care if Paul Newman called with a dozen red roses. (*He takes the mug from James*) Bless you, I need this.
James Where's Vicky?
Henry I left her chuntering down the hill, I couldn't wait to get in fast enough. I don't know why I let myself in for this.
James It was all your idea.
Henry I'm full of brilliant ideas but I don't expect people to carry them out. I've had a lot of ideas about you but it hasn't got me anywhere.

James goes to look out of the shop door

James Is Vicky all right? Where did you leave her?

Henry Top of the High Street. Don't worry about her, she's revoltingly healthy and smug with it. Kept up a stream of merry quips all the way, I could have killed her. Top that up!

Henry holds out his mug and James takes it back to the kitchen to refill it. Henry spots the sauna

Oh, good, you've got it all fixed up. Is it plugged in?

James Yes, it's been on for ten minutes.

Henry I'm tempted to have a go myself. Still, her need is greater than mine. Now don't forget, let me do the ceremonial unveiling.

James O.K. (*He gives Henry his mug again*)

The shop bell jangles

Henry Here comes Madam Zatopek at last. Thump, thump, thump.

James goes back to the kitchen to get another mug

Vicky runs in. She has lost about three stone (no padding), but this is not totally apparent as she is wearing a bulky tracksuit and a towel round her neck. She points at the sheet-covered sauna

Vicky Gosh, what's that?

Henry Never you mind. God, I've never known such a nosey woman. Don't get distracted, keep limbering up. (*He sits in the armchair*)

Vicky stretches and runs on the spot

Vicky James Anderson, you should have come with us. It was marvellous, everything so fresh and pretty covered in frost, you missed a treat.

Henry You didn't. Don't you believe her, it was evil. The dogs were peeing icicles and it was highly dangerous.

Vicky (*laughing*) Oh, yes, James, it was so funny. Cycling round the pond, Isadora here got the end of his scarf caught in the back wheel. You should have heard the fuss he made, all the ducks flew away.

Henry It was a very nasty moment. My neck's never been my best feature, I may have to sue Jaegers.

James smiles and hands Vicky a mug of soup

Vicky Thanks, I can do with this.

Vicky sits on the sofa

Henry No, you don't. Get your paws off that, it's fattening.

Vicky Oh, come on.

Henry Everything's fattening, I don't want you slipping back, stop breathing such greedy gulps of air.

James I've given her the wee mug.

Vicky And it's only Oxo, for God's sake!

Henry Listen to her. Only Oxo! Have you taken a good look at Katie's husband recently?

Vicky All right, I'll just have a sip.

James goes to the kitchen

Henry On your hips be it.

Vicky Henry, what is under that sheet?

Henry You'll find out soon enough. It's a surprise. (*He begins to divest himself of his various garments*) Don't forget, James, tomorrow I want two hot-water bottles strapped on.

Vicky You are a sissy.

Henry So what else is new?

Vicky (*going to the sauna*) It can't be a Christmas present, can it? It's such a big thing.

Henry Hark at the pot calling the kettle black. If you must know, it's your long lost twin sister who's lost her memory and thinks she's the Isle of Wight. Leave it alone and pay attention.

Vicky and Henry go to the wall graph

Let's see, this morning you were nine stone four.

Vicky Yes.

Henry And as there's a week to go before Christmas, you've got to lose another four pounds before Tom gets back.

Vicky Yes, and I'll do it, easily.

Henry goes to the sauna

Henry I've decided to make sure. Having got this far, we might as well be ruthless. Ta tum! (*He dramatically pulls the sheet off the sauna cabinet*)

Vicky What is it? It looks like an outside loo.

Henry It's the latest thing, the Mini-Sauna for Maxi girls.

Vicky I can't afford that. How much did it cost?

Henry Nothing. I've got it on two weeks' appro. After Christmas we sling it back at them and say we're dissatisfied.

Vicky But I'll only sweat it off and put it all back again as soon as I have anything to drink.

Henry Then you won't drink.

Vicky Don't be so daft, I've got to have some moisture.

Henry That has all been taken care of. James Anderson will lay you out in the garden at dawn and you can soak up the dew. Come on, don't hang about, get in.

Vicky You're sure it's safe? Is it wired up properly?

Henry Of course, you don't trust me?

Vicky Frankly, no.

Henry I put James Anderson in it for five minutes yesterday to check.

Vicky What was it like James?

James The heat kinda creeps up on you, but it's not too bad, quite invigorating . . .

Vicky Were you naked?

James Hell, no, I kept my underpants on.

Henry He's not a true Scot, I was shocked.

Vicky And bitterly disappointed. Did you lose any weight, James Anderson?

James I don't know.

Henry Yes, he did, pounds and pounds and half an inch off his sporran. Now, would you mind ceasing this idle chatter and getting in, we're losing all the heat.

Vicky Shall I take my track suit off? I look pretty good, I don't mind.

Henry But I do. Don't forget I was the one who fainted at *Oh Calcutta*— all my worst fears realized.

Vicky I can't get in fully dressed.

Henry Yes, you can, it'll make you sweat more and you won't burn your botty on the seat.

Henry opens the door of the cabinet and Vicky steps in

Vicky I'm going to giggle.

Henry It's a dry heat—no steam. Sit down and keep your head where the hole is.

Vicky sits and Henry closes the doors. James arranges the towel round her neck

Well, what's the verdict?

Vicky It's lovely and warm.

Henry I wish I could say as much for my feet.

James You're sure you're all right, Vicky? Not too hot?

Vicky No, I'm fine. How long do I have to stay in?

Henry A week.

Vicky What!

Henry Houston to control tower, Houston to control tower. One minute to lift off—all systems go—start countdown. Ten, nine, eight, seven . . .

Henry hides behind the sauna

Vicki I'll send you a postcard.

James You're quite comfortable?

Vicky Madly so. I think I'm going to enjoy this.

Henry Not for long. Ha ha! Another victim for Madame La Guillotine. Where's my knitting? Knit one, purl one, drop one and slice.

Vicky Nevair, do you 'ear, nevair. Ze Scarlet Pimp will save me.

Henry Oh, no, I won't. I've got my eye on the young Vicomte de Notre Dame.

Vicky *Sacré bleu!* But 'e 'as, 'ow you say, he has an 'ump on his back?

Henry He'll have two before the night's out.

James goes upstairs

Vicky splutters with laughter

Vicky Oh dear, you've shocked the wee kirk of Scotland.

Henry gets behind the cabinet out of Vicky's eye-line

Henry (*in a Peter Lorre voice*) Forget about him, *liebling*. You see, my pretty thing, I've built this creature from a Meccano set and assorted human bits and bobs. I call him Frank Stein, a little part of him's Jewish.

Vicky Filthy beast.

Henry Ja, ja, but now I need a brain and I'll give you three guesses where that's coming from, *dumpkopf*.

Vicky Henry, don't. Come round where I can see you.

Henry Don't fret, my pretty, you will be immortal.

Vicky Henry, I'm getting too hot, turn it down.

Henry comes and peers at her

Henry Yes, you may have gone a rather nasty pink. Like my mother's twin sets—salmon. I think she calls it.

Vicky I'm sure I've had enough. The temperature's shot up. I'm getting out of here.

Henry bends down at the side of the cabinet, comes to the front of the cabinet and bolts the door

Henry (*in his Peter Lorre voice*) Impossible, my pretty, I'm holding you in. To struggle is useless.

Vicky What?

Henry The brain must be kept at the right temperature.

Vicky Henry, I'm going to scream.

Henry creeps round her to the back; he grabs her from the back

Henry There's no pleasure without pain. You must suffer to be beautiful.

Vicky begins screaming

Vicky Hellllp, James—aaaaaaaaah!

James comes down the stairs at a run

James What is it? What's going on?

Henry Nothing. She's exercising her lungs—reduces the bust.

Vicky James, quick, get me out of here.

James goes at once to the cabinet

Henry Don't touch it, you'll electrocute yourself, you headstrong fool.

James undoes the doors. Vicky falls out into his arms

Vicky Oh, thank God.

James What would you like, tea or brandy? Vicky, tell me.

Henry goes into the living area

Henry Really, what a ridiculous fuss, she hasn't been lost at sea on an open raft, for thirty-six hours, or stuck up a mountain without her woolly drawers, or . . .

James Shut your mouth. Vicky, can I get you anything?

Vicky No, thanks, James, I haven't finished my exercises yet. (*She advances on Henry winding her towel, and begins to chase him round the room, giving him the changing room flick*)

James watches from the kitchen

Henry No, no, no. Ow! No, please that's enough, Vicky. Vicky, a joke's a joke . . . Ow, that hurt—stop it—stop being so hearty . . . Ow! Help! Pax! Control yourself, woman. Ow!

Henry jumps up on the dresser

Vicky You vicious—(*flick*)—horrible—(*flick*)—little—(*flick*)—bugger.
Henry Me vicious? Look at you, snarling like a rabid, aggressive little whippet.

Vicky stops

Vicky Whippet? Did you say whippet?
Henry Yes.
Vicky Aren't they those long, lean, bony dogs that look like small grey-hounds?
Henry I suppose so.

Vicky pulls back her track suit and feels her hips

Vicky All right, Henry, you can get down now. You've made amends.
Henry Thank God for that.
Vicky (*muttering*) Whippet . . .
James I've got some coffee on as well, anybody want a cup?

Henry gets down from the dresser

Henry Yes, please, I need something after my shocking experience—talk about biting the hand that doesn't feed you.
James Vicky?
Vicky Er—yes, I want to take my non-eating pill.

James goes to the kitchen

Henry James Anderson, did you remember the Sunday treat?

Henry sits on the sofa

James Yes.
Henry Well, dish it up. It might put the shrew in a better humour. I've seldom seen such a temper tantrum.
Vicky You'd better get used to them, only fat girls are jolly. And you can get rid of this first thing in the morning. I never want to see it again. (*She kicks the sauna*)
Henry Don't. If you damage it, we'll have to pay for it.
Vicky *You'll* have to pay for it, I haven't signed a thing.
Henry I forged your signature—extremely well.
Vicky I hope you get life. (*She kicks it again*)
Henry You're being very foolish, it would do you a lot of good.
Vicky I shall have nightmares about it as it is.
Henry Come on, you knew I was only joking.
Vicky Like all your jokes, it had the nasty edge of truth about it.

Henry (*being saintly*) What a cynical thing to say. Truth is always good, Victoria.

Vicky Ha. Ha. Ha. Shall I give you a demonstration of the varied powers of the truth? Shall I tell you about yourself, Henry? I promise not to lie, the whole sordid truth and nothing but?

Henry I think we should sue the manufacturers of your slimming pills.

Vicky Eh? They've worked beautifully.

Henry Maybe, but at what a cost! All these sinister side effects.

Vicky All right, I'll buy it. (*She sits in the armchair*)

Henry You've undergone what the courts refer to as a complete change of character, your Honour.

Vicky Balls.

Henry You see. Before you were a sweet, gentle, jolly creature, now you're a hard, callous, pugnacious brute. I'm prepared to give evidence in a dark suit and with a sob in my throat. We'll go halves on whatever you get.

Vicky The only difference is that I'm no longer prepared to let the other girls kick sand in my face.

Henry There's no need to be personal.

Vicky I'm sure of myself, that's all.

Henry And don't we know it. James, where are those cakes?

James Coming.

Vicky What cakes?

Henry Cream cakes. It's Sunday treat time.

James places a tray of coffee and cakes on the table in front of them

There, aren't they lovely. Technically, you have first choice but don't you dare touch Sydney Poitier.

James pours coffee

Vicky Go ahead, I don't want one.

Henry Oh, goody gumdrops. (*He picks up a chocolate éclair*) What do you mean, you don't want one? It's allowed, it's treat time.

Vicky I'm not hungry.

Henry Are you ill?

Vicky No, just not hungry. Oh, I mustn't forget to take my pill.

Vicky takes her coffee and goes upstairs

Henry She's getting positively macabre.

James I thought it was a rotten idea from the first. I don't hold with drugs, they're dangerous things to meddle with. And what's more, I don't think she looks any better either.

Henry You're pretty peculiar, too. You know, it's a funny sensation and one I never thought I would experience, but for the first time in my life I feel completely and utterly normal.

CURTAIN

SCENE 2

The same. Christmas Eve

There is a Christmas tree in one corner, and mistletoe above the stairs. Some paper chains and balloons and other decorations are already up

James is discovered on a chair putting the finishing touches to the Christmas tree. Henry's voice is heard singing from the shop

Henry (*off*) Noël, Noël, Noël, Noëeelle, born is the Queen of Israel . . .

Henry enters loaded with gift-wrapped parcels, which he throws down on the sofa, and takes his coat off

I swear I've aged ten years in the last couple of hours and I can't afford it. I think Oxford Street is a disgrace—I shall write to my M.P. when I find out his name.
James Her name.
Henry Pardon?
James Her name. Our M.P. is a woman.
Henry Oh, I see. All the better, she should know about shopping. She can introduce a Private Member's Bill for the abolition of Oxford Street.
James I thought you liked Selfridge's?
Henry I do, but I hate the people who go there. I was sexually assaulted by two handbags and three umbrellas, one of them with a very strangely shaped handle. I kicked one old cow back and she shrieked like Madame Curie discovering radium, obviously hadn't heard of Women's Lib.
James You're a fool to go into the West End on Christmas Eve.
Henry You're the sneaky type that buys their Christmas presents at the summer sales, aren't you?
James I do try to be sensible. I'm giving everybody book tokens this year.
Henry Oh, oh, what dizzy heights of excitement. I shall certainly froth at the mouth when I open mine. (*He looks up at James*)
Henry You don't look very safe. Would you like me to cling to your thighs?
James No, thanks, I've nearly finished.
Henry What a poor excuse. Mistletoe, James Anderson? I can see I'm going to have to keep a watchful eye on you. I know how wild you northern lads get at festival time—must be your pagan blood.

James gets off the chair and stands back to admire his efforts

James Does it look all right?

Henry gives a quick glance

Henry Lovely, quite lovely. It's like sitting in a Lyons Corner House window. Fetch skinny Liz to look at it, she'll get tears in her beady eyes.
James Vicky's gone to the hairdressers.

James puts up another paper chain

Henry But, of course, it's a big night tonight. The return of Big Tom from foreign parts—that's cheered me up, something to look forward to.

James She said to tell you that she wants the place to herself this evening, we've got to go out before he arrives.

James puts the table and chairs back in position

Henry Well, tough titty for her. I certainly intend to be here after all the work I've put in. I'm not going to miss the denouement, the big climax.

James She was very insistent, told me three times.

Henry She's mad. We'll have a jolly get-together and a few drinks for half an hour, then leave them to it.

James I'm not staying, I think she's got every right to her privacy.

Henry She can't expect privacy. Don't you want to see his legs buckle and his eyes reel from their sockets when he beholds her newfound loveliness?

James No, I've got no interest. She was fine as she was. She was an individual.

Henry Stood out in a crowd, you mean?

James You've changed her.

James moves to collect some holly

Henry That was the whole point of the exercise, you idiot. You've really got no visual taste at all, have you? Believe me she looks stunning. Would you say that it's pure coincidence that she's got all those men hanging round the shop and telephoning all day?

James She's not gone out with any of them.

Henry More's the pity. The silly cow's saving it all for this moronic, glorified paraffin man.

James He has written to her every week.

James puts holly on the dresser

Henry So he's one of nature's pen pals, that would be enough to put me off. People who write a lot are highly suspect in my book and invariably dreary.

James That's a ludicrous statement. You've only got to examine the whole history of literature—even I write a lot.

Henry You are the exception that proves the rule. By the way, have you read any of Tom's letters?

James No, of course I haven't.

Henry It is difficult, isn't it? She doesn't exactly leave them lying about, she's developed a highly suspicious nature. The funny thing is, she never speaks about them either. Most people would read out little titbits. (*In a débutante's voice*) "Oh, poor darling, Tommy's been savaged by a camel," he says, "he had eyeballs for lunch, terribly crunchy apparently".

James I'm very glad she doesn't read out anything like that.

Henry Perhaps he's illiterate, maybe all she gets is a blank sheet of paper with kisses and his thumbprint? Which reminds me, your novel's back again.

Henry rummages in his parcels and gets out a thick envelope which he hands to James, who opens it and reads the enclosed letter, putting down the manuscript

Any joy this time?

James crumples the letter and shoves it in his trouser pocket and goes to fiddle with the Christmas tree. Henry picks up the manuscript

Small wonder with a title like *The Braemar Gathering*. Sounds like a knitting pattern. You should have come to me sooner, my lad, call it *Lust Among the Heather*, design a trendy book jacket, Harry Lauder, starkers and waving his gnarled stick about, it'll go like a bomb.

James It's not that sort of book.

Henry Who cares? They won't find out till after they've bought it, then you can say it was meant to be ironical. (*He flips through the pages*) Angus! You can't have a hero called Angus, unless it's a bull. It's not a sickening, sweet animal story, is it?

James Will you put that down, it's not your property.

Henry Sorry. Sorry. Sorry.

Henry puts the manuscript down. James pretends to put finishing touches to the tree. Pause

Here, why isn't there a fairy on top of that miserable tree?

James I didn't think you'd relish the competition.

Henry Aaaah! What a cruel and vicious thing to say, at Christmas, too. Oh, if you only knew the heartache and the torment of us twilight lot. And it weren't my fault, guvnor, honest, it were me mum's. Always wanted a girl she did, called me Edna and made me wear knickers till I were twenty-three. I never knew no different. Sob, sob, gulp . . .

James Shut up.

Henry I don't think I can, sob, sob.

The shop doorbell jangles

James Vicky's back.

Henry What sharp ears you've got, Grandma.

James and Henry look towards the door

Vicky enters. She carries a shop bag. She has a new hair style. She comes into the room, smiles and takes off her gloves, then her loose-fitting coat. Underneath she wears a new, figure revealing dress. She executes a full turn

Vicky Hello. Well, say something.

James Would you like a cup of tea?

James goes to the kitchen. Henry goes up to her and examines her at arm's length

Vicky Yes, please. Thought I might as well go the whole hog.

Henry You look magnificent, darling, and I'm proud of you. (*He hugs her and lifts her off the floor*)

Vicky Ah, be careful.

Henry lets her go and bends over

Henry You're so right.

Vicky Crumbs, have you done yourself irreparable damage?

Henry sits

Henry Very possibly. Our hip bones clashed. I never knew you had any. Give her a plate of spaghetti, James Anderson, before she castrates the entire male population—I've heard of birth control but this is ridiculous.

Vicky Fool!

James Would you like something to eat, Vicky?

Vicky No, thanks, but I would love a cup of tea.

James Just with lemon, I suppose?

Vicky Please.

Vicky sits in the armchair. James goes back into the kitchen. Henry's panto-mime catches Vicky's attention and she looks up at the decorations

(*Rising*) Oh, James Anderson, the place looks marvellous. Did you do it all yourself?

Vicky moves around to look at the decorations

Henry Cecil Beaton helped. He's a sweetie.

James It was nothing, something to do. Glad you like it, Vicky.

Vicky It's lovely. Thank you, love. Now I really feel it's Christmas—the best one ever. (*She puts her arm round his neck and kisses him*)

James I'll—I'll go and put the kettle on. (*He goes to the kitchen, happy and confused*)

Henry His first kiss, I can't bear it. If this goes on, I shall shed tears and sing a carol.

Vicky looks at the parcels on the sofa

Vicky Gosh, James, you have been busy.

Henry No, he hasn't, those are mine. And you can take your thieving paws off them, your present isn't there, it's being delivered from Fortnum's.

Vicky Fortnum's? How posh.

Henry Yes, a year's supply of chip butties.

Vicky Ah. You little angel, you spoil me. Just for that Mamma's going to give you a great big French kiss. (*She advances on him*)

Henry Don't come near me. Keep away, I had garlic on toast for lunch.

Vicky Then it's going to be very French.

Henry Stop it, it'll end in tears.

Vicky throws herself on him

Vicky I can't help myself, you're looking very lovely tonight.
Henry No, please, Victor, I've got a headache.
Vicky It's not your head I'm after.
Henry No, don't. Ah! Ah!

The telephone rings. Vicky stops

Aren't the Samaritans wonderful—they ring you now.

Vicky picks up the phone

Vicky Four, three, fiv . . . one of those bloody pip, pip, pips . . . Hello? . . . What? . . . Tom! Where are you calling from? . . . How did . . . That's marvellous. I wasn't expecting you till tonight . . . No, no, of course I'm delighted . . . Mmm, yes, so am I . . . No, come right over, it's perfectly all right. Yes, see you—good-bye darling. (*She replaces the receiver*)
Henry Wrong number?
Vicky (*suddenly in top gear*) That was Tom, he's on his way over immediately, he's at the tube station.
James How can he be?
Henry It's obvious, isn't it? He never went to Persia at all. The little darling works at Macfisheries and likes to dream.
Vicky He came back with the managing director in his private jet, then his boss had a car waiting and dropped him off at the station. He's going to be here any minute. (*She darts nervously about the room picking things up*)
Henry Don't get your knickers in a twist. He's not going to catch you with your hair in curlers, you couldn't look lovelier—in fact, I can't wait to see his face.
Vicky What? No. No, you've got to clear out.
Henry No need to shriek like Madame Curie.
Vicky Both of you. Be quick. I must be alone when I see him.

James runs across the room and up the stairs

James (*as he goes*) I'll get my coat, I won't be a minute.

Henry picks up one small parcel and takes it to the tree. Vicky tidies up the kitchen

Vicky Henry, what are you doing?
Henry Tidying up.
Vicky Oh, for Christ's sake. (*She grabs all the parcels and almost chucks them under the tree*)
Henry You should work for British Rail. Do be careful.

Vicky picks up his coat and holds it out for him

Vicky Don't shilly shally, come on.
Henry Perhaps I should wear my raincoat.

Vicky It's a clear day. Get into this. (*She takes his hand and pushes it into a sleeve*)

Henry Ow. All right, all right, don't panic or you'll sweat. It's positively Dickensian being flung out into the snow on Christmas Eve.

James runs down the stairs buttoning up his reefer coat

Vicky nervously tidies the kitchen

James I'm ready. Are you coming, Henry?

Henry Coming where? I've only just got in and I'm certainly not going to sit on the pavement for a couple of hours in this weather. I'll get piles.

Vicky Go and have a coffee somewhere.

Henry Can't I sit in the kitchen if I promise to wear ear-plugs?

James Why don't you come to the pictures with me? We can just catch the early show.

Vicky Perfect. You'll enjoy it.

Henry All right. Where are my gloves?

Vicky In your pocket. Off you go.

Henry and James move towards the door. Then Henry nips into the bathroom

Henry Won't be a minute, must have a pee, it's this cold weather.

Henry exits to the bathroom

Vicky My God, he's doing this deliberately.

James Don't worry, Vicky. Tom can't possibly get here before we go.

Vicky He said it would only take him a few minutes. Damn, why did this have to happen?

James I hope you have a very pleasant evening, Vicky.

Vicky Thank you, James, that's sweet of you. Sorry to push you out like this, but you do understand?

James Aye.

Vicky Oh, where's that bloody Henry?

James nips up the stairs and knocks on the bathroom door

James Come on, Henry, we'll miss the beginning.

Vicky Henry will you get your finger out? James Anderson, do something.

James Henry, if you don't come out I'm going to batter the door down.

Henry opens the door immediately and enters

Henry I never play hard to get.

Vicky There's the exit, use it.

James Come on. (*He opens the main door*)

Henry I do wish you'd both stop fussing. There's plenty of time, he's not superman. Is my hair all right?

Vicky Lovely, careless disarray.
Henry I'm ready then. Good luck.

Henry moves towards the door that James is holding open

Vicky Thank you, have a marvellous time and don't rush back.
Henry Half a sec, I've just remembered something. (*He hurries over to the parcels under the tree*)
Vicky Henry, please!

Henry opens one of the parcels and takes out a large fur hat

Henry I bought myself a pressie and I want to try it out. What do you think?
Vicky Couldn't be more you—stick it on your nut and shove off.

Henry arranges the hat on his head

Henry Has to be at just the right angle or I look like Davy Crockett.
Vicky Stop. Leave it there, that's perfect—terribly Catherine of Russia.
Henry You think so?
Vicky Absolutely, a dead ringer.
Henry O.K. What are we hanging about for? Let's go!
James Wait! I'm not going out with him if he wears that.

James stops at the top of the stairs

Vicky James Anderson, please don't you start.
James People are going to stare.
Henry That's the general idea, you twit.
James I'm sorry, but I refuse to be embarrassed in public.
Vicky It'll be dark in the cinema.
James That's as may be, but we've got to get through the foyer and that's very well lit.
Vicky Buy separate tickets and meet up inside.
James What about the intermission?
Vicky He's not going to keep it on during the film. Are you? Henry, you're not, are you?
Henry No, of course not, the very idea.
Vicky There you are.
James Very well.

Vicky gives a sigh of relief

Henry I shall take it off at once when the gentleman behind me leans forward and says, "Will you kindly remove your hat, madam".
James That does it, I'm going on my own.
Henry I'm joking, you Celtic clot.
James I don't trust you.
Henry How can you say that, James Anderson? I'm wounded, deeply wounded. To think that . . .

Vicky grabs Henry with one hand and James with the other and pushes them through the door

Vicky Shut up the pair of you. I don't care where you go or how you go, but bugger off. (*She goes to the drinks table and pours herself a drink*)

Henry reappears at the door and comes down the steps

Henry Ahem.
Vicky What is it now?
Henry Forgot my handbag.

Vicky picks up a bottle by the neck

Vicky I'm going to kill you.
Henry You don't have a motive.
Vicky I'll choose one afterwards.

The doorbell rings: da, di di di di—dum dum

Henry Ah! Vicky, how dreadful. It looks as if I'm going to see the famous reunion after all, or would you like me to hide under the sofa? I promise to be terribly quiet.

James pokes his head in from the shop

James (*in a whisper*) Vicky, it's Tom. I can see him through the door. What shall I do?
Vicky Let him in.
Henry Yes, do, we don't want him to catch cold.
Vicky On your way out.
Henry Wait. It's going to look awfully rude if we push off the minute he arrives. What will he think?
Vicky He'll think that you're a nice, tactful, self-effacing creature.
Henry The man's not a fool.

The doorbell gives one long ring

Vicky Answer it, James.
James Yes, Vicky.

James exits

Vicky moves towards the stairs

Vicky I'm going upstairs. (*She gives Henry the bottle*)
Henry Excellent idea, you can make an entrance, I'll put some music on.
Vicky And I'm not coming down until you've gone. And that means until I can see you in the street. Good night, Henry.

The shop bell jangles

There are limits to friendship and you've just reached them.

Vicky goes upstairs

Henry comes further into the room and turns to face the door

    Tom enters, bronzed and carrying a bulky holdall

Henry Tom! What a wonderful surprise.
Tom Hello, Henry—like your bonnet.
Henry Thank you. What a sensational tan—looks just like make-up in this light. Make yourself at home, Vicky won't be long.
Tom Good, I can't wait to see her.
Henry Yes, she's—no, I won't spoil it for you. (*He shouts up the stairs*) Vicky, Tom's here barely passing for white. See you later, darling. 'Bye. Don't bother to look out of the window. 'Bye.

    Henry blows Tom a kiss and exits

Tom smiles and shakes his head, sits on the sofa and begins to go through his holdall. He takes out a package and carved box and places them on the coffee-table

    Vicky enters

Vicky Hello, Tom, welcome back.
Tom Vicky, I've . . .
Vicky You're looking marvellous.
Tom So are you; yes, indeed, terrific.
Vicky I said I had a surprise for you.
Tom Yes, but I never dreamt that, that it was anything like this. I—I can't get used to it.
Vicky Neither can I. I still catch myself trying to squeeze through small doors sideways. But I'm still me basically—no internal alteration.
Tom Of course.

They kiss, Tom is the first to pull away and they stand a little awkwardly smiling at each other

    There's quite a difference.
Vicky I'm glad to say. Take your time, sit down and I'll get you a drink. Is it still vodka?
Tom Yes, thank you.
Vicky How was your flight? (*She pours the drink*)
Tom Terrific. The company's private plane. Very grand, we had a stewardess each.
Vicky How posh. Do you want ice with this?
Tom No, that's fine as it is.

Vicky hands him his drink and sits in the armchair

    Thank you, Skol—aren't you having one?
Vicky Heavens, no, that was the first thing I was forced to give up.
Tom Forced to?

Vicky Yes, doctor's orders.

Tom Oh, I see, you've been ill?

Vicky No, at least I had flu last month but then so did everybody else.

Tom But you said that the doctor . . .

Vicky Sorry, no, I meant Doctor Henry. He's as pleased as punch you know—telling everyone he's achieved the world's first body transplant.

Tom I see. You're still letting him run your life.

Vicky No, it was his suggestion, my decision.

Tom Ah . . .

Vicky Do you like our Christmas decorations?

Tom Yes, they're terrific.

Vicky James Anderson did them.

Tom How is he?

Vicky Oh, still writing. (*After a pause*) Well.

Tom Yes.

Vicky Tom, please.

Tom What?

Vicky Do stop looking so worried it'll soon sort itself out, you'll see.

Tom What do you mean?

Vicky This awkwardness between us, it's only natural. After all we're more or less pen pals, aren't we?

Tom That's true.

Vicky I've always thought that words on paper was a rotten way of communication—so one-dimensional. I think you have to know someone for years before you can fully appreciate their letters.

Tom You're right, I suppose. How much weight have you actually lost?

Vicky Three and a half stone so far.

Tom So far? You mean you haven't stopped?

Vicky No. That is on a diet one should always go a little below one's natural weight in order to allow for adjustments later.

Tom I didn't know that.

Pause

Vicky How long are you going to be in England this time, do you know yet?

Tom I'm not sure.

Vicky Well, you're here for the festive season anyway.

Tom Actually, Vicky, I did half promise to spend Christmas with my sister.

Vicky Then you must, Christmas is a family occasion. Where does she live.

Tom Richmond.

Vicky It's very pretty, Richmond.

Tom Yes, it is.

Vicky Is she married?

Tom Yes.

Vicky Any children?

Tom Two, a boy and a girl.

Vicky The perfect combination. It's been a disaster, hasn't it?
Tom Why? Why didn't you write and tell me?
Vicky I didn't think it would matter.
Tom I thought about you every night, looked at your photograph.
Vicky And now I've shattered the likeness, silly me.
Tom I thought you knew.
Vicky How could I?
Tom That night why did you think I stayed?
Vicky Who knows? Kindness, pity for a poor fat girl, a cheap hotel room. I didn't mean that.
Tom I wrote every week.
Vicky I know you did.
Tom I'm afraid I'm not very good at expressing myself.
Vicky I had noticed—ha, ha—I'm sorry I'm not laughing at you—just the situation—pretty hilarious if you think about it. Talk about wasted effort, Jesus.

Vicky rises and moves away

Tom You don't think that perhaps you could perhaps you could— put . . .
Vicky No, I'll make bloody sure I don't. This is me, I like the way I am and I haven't enough pioneering spirit to be a sixteen stone sex symbol.
Tom Very well, I'm sorry truly sorry, Vicky. (*He rises*)
Vicky So am I. Would you like another drink before you go?

Vicky sits again

Tom No, thanks. Those are for you—some jewellery and things.
Vicky How kind of you. What a pretty box.
Tom Just some Persian sweetmeats.
Vicky Desperately fattening, I'm sure.
Tom Crushed almonds and sesame seeds. Vicky, is there anything I can say?
Vicky No.

Tom exits

Vicky remains still for a moment, then picks up Tom's presents and moves to the Christmas tree. She turns on the radio. Then she goes to the dresser and searches for a pair of scissors and goes to the stairs

Vicky exits upstairs and returns with the fat dress

She rips one arm out, picks up the scissors and starts to cut, as—

the CURTAIN falls

SCENE 3

The same. Later that evening

When the CURTAIN *rises, the room is in darkness except for the Christmas tree lights. Vicky is hunched up in a chair in the dark*

The shop bell jangles

Henry (*off*) Ssssh! Come on—that's it, take it easy—you're almost there.

The door to the room is opened by Henry, who stands in the doorway

Let go of that and mind the step. I'll catch you.

James, drunk, rushes and falls into the room

Will you please be quiet, James Anderson, they'll think I'm dragging something back.

James I may have broken my leg.

Henry You shouldn't wear such high heels. Get up, I'm not going to carry you and I refuse to give you a thrill by walking over you after the way you've behaved. (*He pulls James to a sitting position on the stairs and edges past him*) Be a good boy and stay there till I put a light on. (*He comes into the room*) Dizzy cow's gone to bed and left the tree on. (*He puts the light on*)

Vicky Oh, no, she hasn't.

Henry Aaaah! What a perfectly beastly thing to do. (*He takes off his hat and strokes it*) Made all the hairs on my hat stand on end.

Vicky I'm sorry, I'm sorry.

Henry Oh, Lord. Give us a hand, Vicky. He may not look it but he weighs, must have big bones.

Vicky puts another light on. Henry bends over James, and Vicky joins him

Vicky Poor James Anderson, what's nasty Henry done to you this time?

Henry You won't get any sense out of him. Grab an arm and pull.

They each take an arm and tug. James rises a few inches

He's stuck.

Vicky James Anderson, don't sag, push.

Henry That's it, push. Push for Vicky, push, push.

Vicky You sound like a midwife.

They get James to his feet

Henry That's it. Mrs Anderson, you've got a lovely boy.

Vicky Now what? We can't hold him up all night.

Henry Put him on the sofa till I get my breath back.

Vicky O.K.

Henry Come and sit down, Jamsie. Lovely Vicky will look after you and make you better.

They get James to the sofa, where he slumps

Vicky I've never seen him like this. What happened? (*She sits on the sofa*)
Henry What didn't? It's been an absolutely frantic evening.

Henry sits in the armchair

Vicky Has it? How was the film?
Henry Ghastly. James Anderson sulked all through it and wouldn't buy me any nuts in the interval.
James Ooohhh.
Vicky Where did you booze? I take it the Odeon hasn't suddenly got a drinks licence?
Henry That was something else. He's been acting funny all evening, so I suggested we pop across the road to the local for a seasonal nightcap where he starts knocking back the scotch as if it were Hogmanay, slumps quickly into some sort of morose Celtic fit and when they call time he twitches and knocks my Guinness all over the tart sitting next to him.
James I said I was sorry.
Henry He did, too. This slag had on the most ghastly number in silver, open work, crochet, can you imagine the mess?
Vicky Don't!
Henry Luckily, she was also sporting a corsage of plastic orchids and I insisted it was the sight of them that had made James Anderson twitch. She shrieked a bit . . .
Vicky Like Madame Curie discovering radium?
Henry Near enough, but everybody else laughed and I managed to get James out before the Irish navvy she was with came out of the gents. So here we are. What about your evening, how did that go and why are you sitting here playing Fireside Sal?
Vicky I've been waiting up for you.
Henry Aaaah, aren't you nice. (*He bends and kisses her forehead*)

She gives him a hefty kick on the shins

(*He hops on one leg*) Ow! Bloody hell. What did you do that for?
Vicky Because it made me feel a lot better.
Henry I don't think that's a good enough reason.
Vicky Reasons are not popular with me this evening.
Henry Oh. Where's your friend Tom? He didn't have a heart attack, did he?
Vicky No, there wasn't time; he didn't stay long.
Henry What a shame. When's he coming back?
Vicky He's not.
James Good.
Henry But why, what happened?
Vicky Nothing much. He appeared to think that I was some sort of balloon that could be blown up to size at will.

Henry What?
Vicky I mean he likes fat women.
Henry St Teresa of the Roses!
James I said it was stupid but no-one listens to me.
Henry Are you sure you haven't got it all wrong, what did he actually say?
Vicky Nothing very much but the message was loud and clear. Fat is
  beautiful.
Henry Oh, love, how awful—I am sorry—did he faint when he saw you?
Vicky Not quite. But he did have the same glazed look of horror James
  Anderson gets when a soufflé doesn't rise.
Henry It's all so bleeding unfair, why couldn't he have met you when
  you were huge?
Vicky He did.
Henry Oh, yes. Well, pity he wasn't a foot fetishist, something simple
  we could have coped with.

Henry sits in the armchair

Vicky It's not the end of the world. Not even very suprising if you think
  about it. Men seem to specialize more than women, they categorize
  themselves into leg or tit enthusiasts. Some adore virgins, some are
  obsessed with whores. One in twenty pursues men and the vast majority
  never find the time or opportunity to discover what they want. It's all
  part of the merry cavalcade called Life. (*She rises and moves away. After
  a pause*) There's no need to maintain a respectful silence. Do laugh
  quietly amongst yourselves if you want to.
Henry What a rotten anticlimax, you were meant to live happily ever
  after. It's obviously high time I retired as resident fairy godmother, I'm
  handing in my wand.
Vicky It was my fault, I let it get out of proportion. I hardly knew the
  man and if I'm truthful, I did find his letters boring—short, repetitive
  little sentences that I kidded myself meant he was honest and un-
  complicated.
Henry There aren't many of those around. Let's face it, Tom was dreary,
  nowhere near good enough for you. The fact that he's hooked on moun-
  tains of flesh is the most interesting thing about him. I wonder how it
  started, do you think he had a vast nanny or an overweight teddy bear?
Vicky I handled the whole thing badly, I got annoyed and over-reacted.
  He's very naïve basically, I'm afraid I may have hurt him.
James You were quite right, Vicky.
Vicky No, I hope he gets in touch again so that I can be more sympathetic.
  It's not his fault.
Henry Poor thing, doomed to a life of hanging about outside weight-
  watchers' classes.
Vicky He'll make some girl very happy. (*She sits on the sofa*)
Henry (*after a pause*) You know, once, many years ago I read on a wall
  "I want a ginger-haired man with no ears". I've always hoped it was a
  joke.
Vicky Oh, it must have been, it's awful. I mean you could search for your

whole life and not find one. It doesn't bear thinking about. Suppose
you finally found one and he didn't fancy you? What would you do?

Henry Even worse, what if after years of private inquiry agents, success
was imminent, the prize within your grasp, with an eager smile and
trembling hands you knock on his door, he opens it—and he's gone
bald!

Vicky No, no, don't, stop it. It's got to be a joke.

James Has it? What if you yourself were ginger-haired and without ears?

Vicky I'd never go out.

Henry I would knit myself some very close-fitting hats.

Vicky And you'd miss your big chance.

Henry It wouldn't be the first time, would it? I know, let's write to
Woman's Own for advice.

They both collapse into giggles. James rises to his feet

James Prisoners, that's all you are. Prisoners of a bourgeois society.

Henry Gawd! He's had a rush of blood to the head.

Vicky edges up on the sofa

James You're trapped by the very false images that you profess to despise.
Men are virile, women are beautiful, walk down any street and see how
many fall into that category—children are innocent, workers are real,
policemen are wonderful—and if you don't fit, cover up, pretend,
delude yourself—point the finger at the other person, it can't be you
that's causing the smell—ignore your own reflection 'cause you don't
feel like that inside—you're one of the Golden people—your race,
religion, football team and car is the best—tiny faults naturally but
nothing to worry about, we are human after all, none of us is perfect—
when you walk through a storm keep your head up high and you won't
see the shit that you're treading in.

Henry Thank you, we'll let you know.

Vicky Do you feel all right, James?

James I've loved you like a sister.

Henry Which one of us is he talking to?

Vicky Shut up, Henry. That's terribly sweet of you, James, and I'm very
fond of you too. Sit down, and I'll make us all some tea in a minute.

James It's a pure love, totally unaffected by what size you are or what you
look like.

Henry Fine. She'll call you when she's grown a moustache.

James I'm disappointed in both of you, it's time I left. I promised myself
that I'd go as soon as I had a book accepted for publication, so it's an
ironic coincidence.

Henry Someone's going to publish your book! (*He rises*)

James Aye.

Vicky gets up and goes to James quickly and hugs him

Vicky James, how smashing! That's absolutely marvellous news. I'm
delighted for you, love. We must do something to celebrate.

Henry (*holding out his hand to James*) Congratulations, I'm terribly pleased.

Vicky Have we got any champagne anywhere?

James (*shouting*) Stop it! Cooking sherry would be more appropriate.

Henry What do you mean?

James My novel has been turned down by every publishing house in the country.

Vicky But you said . . .

James Aye, I've had a book accepted—a cook book, a bloody cook book.

Vicky Oh, well, it's a start, a splendid start.

Henry You'll make tons more money. It will sell like hot cakes.

James It's quite a blow to have your innermost thoughts rejected and your recipes accepted.

Vicky Don't talk so daft. Come and have a drink.

James No. No, I won't be embarrassing you further. I'll be leaving in the morning. I just wanted you to know, that's all. Good night. (*He walks to the stairs*)

Vicky Darling, think it over, it's Christmas Day tomorrow.

Henry The trains won't be running.

James turns

James I'll—I'll put the turkey in before I go.

Vicky Thank you, James, thank you very much.

James exits

Vicky turns to Henry

Oh dear.

Henry Don't worry, he's young. Poor sod, his first big moment and he has to screw it up.

Vicky I don't think he'll remember much about it in the morning.

Henry Good, we'll manage to persuade him that he's a cross between Hemingway and Barbara Cartland.

Vicky Yes, we must—and it is exciting for him.

Henry Some people are never satisfied. Did he ever let you read his novel?

Vicky Yes.

Henry What was it like?

Vicky Awful, really awful.

Henry Oh. Want some coffee?

Henry goes to the kitchen. He puts on the light on the dresser

Vicky Mmm, that would be nice.

Henry plugs the kettle in

Instant will do.

Henry No other thought had crossed my mind. Do you want a biccy, Vicky?

Vicky No, thanks. (*She follows him into the kitchen*)

Henry picks up a packet of biscuits and tries to get the wrapping off

Henry One of these days, someone is going to starve to death surrounded by pre-packed, pre-wrapped preposterous food that they have been unable to get their laughing gear round.

Vicky Give it me. I never had any trouble in the old days.

Henry But you had a great natural talent—I've seen you open a tin of peaches with a safety pin before now.

Vicky You won't be any good till they put zips on everything. (*She opens the packet and hands it back*)

Henry Thanks, glad to see you haven't lost your touch.

Vicky begins to prepare the coffee

Vicky I'll make the coffee, too, or we'll be here all night.

Henry opens the pedal bin to throw biscuit wrapping in, but he bends and runs his hand through some small shreds of blue material

Henry Darling, you know it's not in my nature to pry, but what the hell is this?

Vicky The fat dress—I cut it up.

Henry How could you? What a beastly thing to do.

Vicky What are you talking about?

Henry It's horrible. A faithful friend of many years standing, who never complained, always there in an emergency, now viciously torn to shreds in an act of cheap symbolism. Alas, poor fat dress, I knew her well, Horatio, a garment of infinite stretch . . .

Vicky If you feel that strongly about it, let's have a formal cremation in the garden tomorrow with fireworks, cymbals and floral tributes.

Henry You forget, this is a smokeless zone. It'll have to be Golders Green again, I'll ring in the morning and make an appointment.

Vicky They won't allow fireworks.

Henry They will if I tell them she's Chinese.

Vicky I don't think they'll believe you.

Henry, still letting the shreads run through his fingers, picks out the label of the dress

Henry They'll have to, I've just found her birth certificate. Du Barry Fashions. WXXXXX. Made—pin your lugholes back, Madam—made in Hongkong.

Vicky It's not true?

Henry See for yourself.

Vicky takes the label

Vicky Du Barry Fashions, Hongkong—I'll keep this as a souvenir. (*She sits at the table*)

Henry throws the pieces of dress in the pedal bin

Henry You should have kept the whole dress, it might have come in useful. The fact is potentially you're a fat lady and you always will be. Disaster will never be further away than the nearest packet of biscuits or box of chocolates. Can you live with that for the rest of your life?

Vicky That's what I want to find out and I think I have to find it out alone. Sit down, Henry, drink your coffee.

Henry sits at the table with her

When Tom left this evening I was disappointed and a bit annoyed but I wasn't shattered—none of my usual reactions, I didn't rush to the nearest piece of cake, and suddenly I realized why—I'm a different person, Henry, externals do affect one's way of thinking and I think it would be impossible for me not to change my way of living.

Henry Alone?

Vicky I'd like to try. I never have and I'm twenty-nine.

Henry In a good light who isn't?

Vicky Before you there was my father.

Henry He was somewhat older.

Vicky You know what I mean.

Henry You do realize that it's everyone's favourite fantasy, to cut loose, burn everything and start afresh?

Vicky One or two succeed.

Henry You've got a very slim chance. What are you planning to do, sell the shop and sail for the South Seas tomorrow to paint and chop your ear off?

Vicky I wasn't thinking of anything so drastic—or so immediate.

Henry gets up and goes to the living area

Henry You should. Few people find the courage to begin again. Usually old lives vanish or wither away and if you're lucky something fills the gap. If not, you plod on dragging the corpses of past glories, old friends and happy loves with you to the grave. No, you're right and I feel a certain pride in you. I didn't think it would be so soon. You can manage without crutches, what you don't need throw away. (*He sits on the sofa*)

Vicky I shall always need friends. (*She follows Henry in*)

Henry You don't have to live with friends, in fact it's better not to, they last longer. I'll start looking for a flat right away.

Vicky There's lots of time, I don't want to push you out. I only meant that we should think about it over the next six months or so, gradually get used to the idea. (*She sits in the armchair*)

Henry And drift towards another *status quo*? No, you've got to do it now, Vicky, risk being bored and unhappy or you may find that you've joined the little band of women that either through fear or necessity surround themselves with non-threatening or non-functioning males. Take a good look at the women who've settled for that, they're even more hysterical than those who curl up with a cat or a parrot or poodle.

Vicky (*after a pause*) You won't go miles away, you'll find somewhere close? I can help with the money side.

Henry Darling, don't worry, I shall move in next door if I can, be the perfect neighbour, peer from behind the lace curtains, bang on the walls and drill spy holes if you make too much noise in bed, write countless poison pen letters—you won't feel neglected.

Vicky That's nice to know.

Henry And what about James Anderson? Do we find him a place or do we tie a haggis to his feet and drop him in the river?

Vicky I'd still like him to run the shop, if he wants to, and he isn't too busy collecting recipes.

Henry That's settled then, he can move in with me, in a purely platonic sense of course.

Vicky As long as you truly believe that, I'd hate to see you bashing your head against a brick wall—because he isn't.

Henry Don't teach granny to suck eggs, granny's known from the beginning, but where else would I find such a good housewife and cook?

Vicky Pretty rotten future for him.

Henry He'll find his own way—in time. And then there'll be one.

Vicky Never, some new fresh-faced acolyte will appear.

Henry Acolyte? I don't think you know the meaning of half the words you use. Come on. (*He gets up, holds out his hand to pull Vicky up*) Time you were in bed, my girl.

Vicky Cheeky!

The church bells start to ring. They stop to listen and smile at each other. Henry dashes to the tree and picks a small present which he hands to her

Henry Time for your present. Open it. Not very Christmassy, I'm afraid, but appropriate.

Vicky tears the wrapping off and takes out a very small bikini

Vicky Oh, Henry, it's super. Thank you. It's what I've always wanted.

Henry I had to get it from the large child department.

Vicky You bloody, gorgeous liar. (*She throws her arms around him*) Merry Christmas, Henry.

Henry Happy New Year, Victoria. (*He gives her a long kiss*)

Vicky Why, Mr Simmonds, I didn't know you cared.

Henry Kindly extinguish that tiny spark of doubt at the back of your beady little eyes. There's no reason to raise your hopes, because . . .

Vicky I know, I'm standing under the mistletoe.

Henry Exactly, you bold hussy.

Vicky Still, you did put a lot of time and effort into changing me, the least I can do is to try and return the compliment. I'll be along to your room later, don't lock the door.

Henry If you can get past the wardrobe, the sawn floor boards, the electrified wire fence, and the Doberman Pincher—you have a very slim chance.

Vicky Pity.

Henry But there it is. Ask me again when I'm eighty, you might find your luck's changed.

Vicky Don't think I won't. (*He kisses her gently on the forehead*)

Henry Go on, you go and use the bathroom first.

Vicky Good night, Henry.
Henry Good night, Vicky.

Vicky exits to the bathroom

Henry stands thinking for a moment. He moves to the sofa, sits, picks up his coffee, and begins to drink, as—

the CURTAIN falls

FURNITURE AND PROPERTY LIST

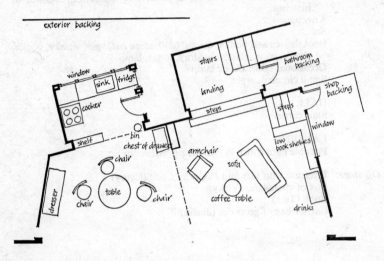

ACT I

SCENE 1

On stage: **KITCHEN**

Cooker. *On and beside it:* saucepan with milk, electric kettle. *In oven:* casserole

Fridge. *In it:* salad dressing, tarragon, spam, tomatoes, lettuce, parsley, ice bucket and cubes, plate of cakes and éclair

Sink (practical). *On draining-board:* rack with plates, cloths, towels

Working surface, shelves, racks. *On them:* fruit bowl with apples, toaster with toast, coffee-pot with coffee, serving ladle, salad bowl, servers, mugs, milk jug, pinger. *In drawers:* knives, forks, spoons

Bread bin. *On top:* bread basket and loaf, wrapped packet of biscuits, jar of Nescafé

Pedal bin

On back door: kitchen roll, butcher's apron

DINING AREA

Dresser. *On it:* mirror, lamp, dressing. *In drawer:* scissors

Chest of drawers. *On top:* telephone, radio, lamp, plants. *In drawers:* flippers, etc., pyjamas, cleaning things, dusters, Christmas decorations

Circular table. *On it:* Book, *Guardian* newspaper, toast in rack, butter, marmalade, cornflakes, milk jug, sugar bowl and spoon, 2 plates, knives, 2 mugs, cereal bowl and spoon
3 matching chairs

LIVING-AREA
Coffee-table. *On it:* ashtray, 2 packets of cigarettes, 2 boxes of matches
Armchair
Sofa
Bookshelves and books. *On top* (*downstage end*): gin, whisky, vodka, sherry, wine, glasses, ashtray, tongs, lamp
Occasional table. *On it:* lamp
Small circular carpet

HALL
Stair carpet

LANDING
Possible light souce in wall facing bathroom

Off stage: Briefcase with files and Highway Code (**Henry**)
Box of chocolates (**Vicky**)
Book (**Tom**)
Carrier bag of groceries (**James**)

SCENE 2

Set: Vicky's handbag on sofa
Book on dining-table

Off stage: Evening paper (**Henry**)
Nail file (**Vicky**)

SCENE 3

Strike: Plates, knives, forks, bread basket, casserole
Dirty glass
Evening paper

Set: Fluffy toy on armchair
Mug of coffee and *Weekly Review Supplement* on coffee-table
Sunday Times and coloured section on dining-table
Coffee ready for pouring in kitchen

Off stage: Bunch of flowers and card in envelope (**James**)

ACT II

SCENE 1

Strike: All dirty dishes and glasses
             Vicky's bag
             Fluffy toy

Set: Kitchen tidy and dining-table clear
             Christmas cards on drinks shelf and elsewhere
             Soup in saucepan
             Pieces of fat dress in pedal bin
             2 mugs for James to pour out soup
             Wall chart and streamer "Lose a Ton for Tom"
             Sauna and cloth
             Clean glasses for drinks
             Radio on working surface

Off stage: Towel **(Vicky)**

SCENE 2

Strike: Sauna
             Coffee-tray
             Wall chart and streamer

Set: Christmas tree with decorations and lights
             Radio back on chest of drawers
             Holly behind sofa
             Various Christmas decorations, including mistletoe

Off stage: Carrier with various parcels including hat, bikini, Christmas cards
                  and manuscript with letter in envelope **(Henry)**
             Holdall with carved box and parcel **(Tom)**
             Fat dress **(Vicky)**

SCENE 3

Strike: Fat dress
             Scissors

LIGHTING PLOT

Property fittings required: kitchen and hall pendants, 3 lamps, Christmas tree
    lights
Interior. A flat. The same scene throughout

ACT I, Scene 1. Morning
To open: General effect of sunny August day
No cues

ACT I, Scene 2. Evening
To open: All lamps and interior lighting on
No cues

ACT I, Scene 3. Morning
To open: As Scene 1
No cues

ACT II, Scene 1. Day
To open: General effect of winter daylight
No cues

ACT II, Scene 2. Night
To open: As Act I, Scene 2
No cues

ACT II, Scene 3. Night
To open: Christmas tree lights only on

Cue 1	**Henry** switches on living area pendant	(Page 54)
	Snap on pendant and covering lights	
Cue 2	**Vicky** switches on lamp	(Page 54)
	Snap on remaining living area lighting	
Cue 3	**Henry** switches on kitchen lights	(Page 58)
	Snap on kitchen pendant, lamp, and covering spots	

EFFECTS PLOT

ACT I

SCENE 1

Cue 1   **Vicky:** ". . . apologizing all the time."   **(Page 11)**
Shop bell jangles

SCENE 2

Cue 2   **After CURTAIN rises**   **(Page 15)**
Shop bell jangles

Cue 3   **Henry:** ". . . with thy thighs and . . ."   **(Page 18)**
Doorbell rings

Cue 4   **Vicky:** ". . . like me, they don't."   **(Page 20)**
Doorbell rings

Cue 5   **Henry exits**   **(Page 20)**
Doorbell rings

Cue 6   **Henry:** ". . . well chosen, subtle questions."   **(Page 22)**
Doorbell rings—special ring

Cue 7   **Henry:** "Buzz."   **(Page 28)**
Kitchen pinger sounds

SCENE 3

Cue 8   **As CURTAIN rises**   **(Page 29)**
Church bells

Cue 9   **Henry:** "Oh good, it's Sunday."   **(Page 29)**
Church bells stop

Cue 10   **Henry:** ". . . all that excess weight."   **(Page 30)**
Doorbell rings

Cue 11   **James exits**   **(Page 30)**
Shop bell jangles

Cue 12   **James:** ". . . left the country."   **(Page 31)**
Shop bell jangles

ACT II

SCENE 1

| Cue 13 | As CURTAIN rises | (Page 36) |
| | *Radio music* | |

| Cue 14 | After CURTAIN up | (Page 36) |
| | *Telephone rings* | |

| Cue 15 | James switches off radio | (Page 36) |
| | *Music off* | |

| Cue 16 | James switches on radio | (Page 36) |
| | *Music on* | |

| Cue 16 | As James switches on radio | (Page 36) |
| | *Shop bell jangles* | |

| Cue 17 | James switches off radio | (Page 36) |
| | *Music off* | |

| Cue 18 | James: "O.K." | (Page 37) |
| | *Shop bell jangles* | |

SCENE 2

| Cue 19 | Henry: ". . . sob, sob." | (Page 45) |
| | *Shop bell jangles* | |

| Cue 20 | Henry: "No, don't. Ah! Ah!" | (Page 47) |
| | *Telephone rings* | |

| Cue 21 | Vicky: "I'll chose one afterwards." | (Page 50) |
| | *Doorbell rings—special ring* | |

| Cue 22 | Henry: "The man's not a fool." | (Page 50) |
| | *Doorbell rings—one long ring* | |

| Cue 23 | Vicky: "Good night, Henry." | (Page 50) |
| | *Shop bell jangles* | |

| Cue 24 | Vicky turns on radio | (Page 53) |
| | *Music—continue to end of Scene* | |

SCENE 3

| Cue 25 | After CURTAIN up | (Page 54) |
| | *Shop bell jangles* | |

| Cue 26 | Vicky: "Cheeky!" | (Page 61) |
| | *Church bells—continue to end of Scene* | |